We urgently need in the pulpits of the world a new generation of Simeons who, like him, will expound Scripture with faithfulness, passion and relevance. May this new edition of Handley Moule's famous biography inspire many, as it inspired me.

John Stott

Charles Simeon (1759-1836) left an indelible impression upon his generation. Educated at Eton and then King's College, Cambridge, he was ordained before he was twenty-three years old.

Simeon was the minister of Holy Trinity Church, Cambridge for fifty-four years. But his appointment initially was met with considerable opposition from his parishioners, and it continued unabated for ten years. He endured the opposition and came to be recognised as a great preacher, learned teacher and guide, philanthropist, and discipler of younger men intending to enter the ministry.

He became the object of great personal respect and of very wide influence in the church of his time. A considerable amount of the revived consciousness of corporate life in the church was due to his persistent work and witness. It is possible that the Church of England never had a more loving and devoted son and servant than Charles Simeon.

CHARLES SIMEON

Handley Moule

Christian Focus

The author of this biography was Handley Moule (1841-1920). In 1881 he became the first principal of Ridley Hall Theological College, Cambridge and in 1899 Norrisian professor of divinity. In 1901 he became Bishop of Durham. In addition to this biography, he wrote expositions and commentaries on the New Testament epistles, as well as devotional books.

This biography was first published in 1892 and the reader should bear this in mind when the author refers to current events. A small degree of editing has been done to the text.

© Christian Focus Publications
ISBN 1 85792 310 3

Published in 1997 by Christian Focus Publications, Geanies House, Fearn, Ross-shire, IV20 1TW, Great Britain.

Cover design by Donna Macleod

Contents

Chapter 1

Family and School

Charles Simeon was born at Reading, September 24, 1759. As a boy of nine he was sent to Eton, and was elected there on the foundation. At nineteen he went up with a Scholarship to King's College, Cambridge, and succeeded in due course to a Fellowship, which he held till his death. He was ordained Deacon in 1782, and Priest in 1783. In 1782 he was made Minister, or Perpetual Curate, of the Church of the Holy Trinity in Cambridge; a benefice which was originally a Vicarage of the Abbey of Dereham, and of which, after the suppression of the Abbey, and until the year 1867, the Bishop appointed the Minister. In that pastorate he lived and laboured for just fifty-four years, through many vicissitudes of good report and evil, amidst serious and complicated difficulties, and with results which were felt far and wide. He died November 13, 1836, in his rooms in King's College, and was buried six days later in the great vault beneath the pavement of the antechapel.

We may notice that Simeon's life was almost exactly contemporary with that of his illustrious friend and fellow Cantabrigian, William Wilberforce, who was born in 1759 and died in 1833. William Pitt the younger began his shorter life also in 1759; but Pitt, an undergraduate at fifteen, had left Cambridge before Simeon entered. Another famous name of 1759 is Richard Porson. Like Simeon, and along with him, Porson was on the foundation of Eton, and he took his Bachelor's degree (from Trinity College) in 1782. Simeon outlasted the great Greek scholar seven and twenty years, surviving from a Cambridge which had only recently lost Gray, and was still full of living traditions of Bentley, into a Cambridge which already felt the influence of Sedgwick, Whewell and Julius Hare. Measured on the line of English history, his life extended from the last months of George the Second almost to the accession of Victoria; from 'the year of victories', the year of Wolfe's triumph at Quebec, though the whole course of the American War of Independence, and the campaigns of the French Revolution, till Waterloo was already a memory and the Thirty Years Peace was drawing to its close. In the line of English literature, he travelled from the period of Johnson, Burns and Cowper, to a time when Coleridge had already passed away, and the Lake School was on its way to literary victory, and the first writings of Macaulay and of Tennyson were abroad. And in the line of English religious history, he was born only twenty years after the definite rise of Methodism, and died nine years after the publication of the *Christian Year*, and only nine years before the secession of Newman to the Church of Rome.

Such parallels and comparisons are always interesting and often important in the study of a long and powerful life; for the man who gives out a large influence, continuous and operative through many years, must himself feel and assimilate much of the influence of his time. Yet it is plain to the reader of Simeon's story that he was one of those who are not highly sensitive to contemporary currents of action and thought. Partly by a peculiar concentration and independence of character, partly by a lack of the purely literary instinct, but most of all by an absolutely disinterested and single-minded devotion to 'one thing, followed along a line which for him was drawn very distinctly, and in a certain sense narrowly, by the providence of God', Simeon passed his seventy-seven years very much more as a giver than a receiver of influence. We look in vain in his diaries, sermons, or letters for a large reflection of the innumerable interest of his period. Everything betokens a mind alert and vigorous, an observer full of clear intelligence, a man to whom nothing human was indifferent. But when he sat down to write, he wrote very much as Wesley had written before him, Wesley the all-observant and all-reading; like a man whose pen had little time for anything off the line of his public or private Christian ministry.

Family

Charles Simeon's father was Richard Simeon, Esq., the son and grandson of successive Vicars of Bucklebury, in Berkshire, and descended directly from the Simeons of Oxfordshire, a house which had given a wife to John Hampden. His mother was Elizabeth Hutton, daughter of a family from which came two Archbishops to the see of York, each of them a Matthew Hutton, the former under Elizabeth [the First], the latter under George the Second. When this is said about Mrs Simeon, all is recorded which can be gathered either from memoirs of her son or from the recollections of his yet surviving friends. He was her fourth and youngest son and child; and perhaps she died before his memory. In any case his early life seems to have lacked altogether a mother's influence, whether felt in its living power as the Wesleys felt it, and the elder Venn, or in the deep pathos of a remembered loss, such as Cowper knew. Richard Simeon himself was an upright man, commanding the deference of his son rather than his affection, holding religion in what is known as respect, but certainly not fostering its spirit and power in his family. He

survived till Charles' twenty-fifth year. Of his three elder
sons the first, Richard, died young, in 1782. The second, John,
was Fellow of All Souls, a Master in Chancery, one of the
managers of the private property of George the Third, and
Member for Reading, and was created a Baronet in 1815.[1]
The third, Edward, was one of the Directors of the Bank, a
successful and wealthy merchant.

Eton

Of Charles' Eton life a few fragmentary recollections are
preserved. The boy was full of muscle and agility; he could
'jump over half a dozen chairs in succession, and snuff a
candle out with his feet.' Quite early in life he became, what
he was almost to the last, an excellent horseman, brave and
dexterous, and as good a judge of a horse as if he had been
born in Yorkshire. Along with energy and courage he showed,
as also in later life, a side of oddity, better described as
unconventionality in acts and habits, a rare thing in school-
boys. The American War was raging (it was in 1776) and a
national fast-day was enjoined. Simeon, in the words of his
own reminiscence, 'thought that if there was one who had
more displeased God than others, it was I. To humble myself
therefore before God appeared to me a duty of immediate
and indispensable necessity. Accordingly I spent the day in
fasting and prayer. But I had not learned the happy art of
"washing my face and anointing my head, that I might not
appear unto men to fast". My companions noticed the change
in my deportment, and immediately cried out (did Porson,
who never loved Simeon, suggest the Greek?) ...Greek words

---

1. The title of baronet had been held by members of the Simeon family
almost from the foundation of the order.

Woe, woe unto you, hypocrites; by which means they soon dissipated my good desires, and reduced me to my former state of thoughtlessness and sin. I do not remember that these good desires ever returned during my stay at school.'

Yet an old schoolfellow, J.H. Mitchell, who survived him, says that his habits 'became peculiarly strict from that period, and that he was known, not without ridicule on the part of those who knew, to keep an alms-box, into which he put money for the poor whenever conscience accused him of wrong in word or deed'.

Eton at that time was no favourable seminary for virtue. The morals of schools in our own day occasion often grave anxiety to those who look beneath the surface. But surely few fathers now would deliberately say what Simeon said in his later age, that he would be tempted to take the life of a son rather than let him see the vice he had seen at Eton. And his own conduct at school, according to his own estimate, was in some respects deplorable; not, however, as far as I can gather, in the sense of impure talk or habits, but in that of ungovernable temper and extravagance in spending.

King's College, Cambridge

From Eton he passed to King's College, January 29, 1779, bringing with him the Etonian's sound Latin scholarship, but not a great store of Greek. At no time of life did he effectually mend this latter defect; and indeed even in academic circles, in his younger days, Greek was far less accurately known than Latin, save by a few students. Of Simeon's undergraduate studies scarcely a line of record remains, indeed nothing beyond the notice that he was lectured in Pearson's *Exposition of the Creed* and the *Ethics of Aristotle*, and took a strong interest in both courses. The privileges of his College, privileges which brought little benefit to the illustrious foundation, positively debarred him from the stimulus of public examinations. But his afterwork seems to indicate that he never could be quite idle; and scarcely had he entered King's when, as we shall see presently, the most powerful of all incitements to a life of duty took full possession of his energetic will.

It was into a Cambridge very different from the present that Simeon was introduced. Externally, the place was a country town of some ten thousand inhabitants, exclusive of perhaps a thousand members of the University. It was poorly appointed as a town; no street lamps of any kind were used for years before 1779, and carriages could traverse only with difficulty some parts even of the main thoroughfare. Tracts or patches of moor and fenland surrounded it everywhere, almost at the gates of the outlying colleges. The now densely-peopled suburb of Barnwell was a small village in the fields. King's College, as the young scholar found it, possessed indeed its glorious Chapel, and already beside the Chapel stood the fine structure of Portland stone, Gibbs' Building, otherwise the Fellows' Building, in which the newcomer was soon to lodge and was at last to die. But otherwise the difference was great between the past aspect of the College and the present. The street now called King's Parade, then High Street, was bordered, on the college side of it, by old-world shops and dwelling-houses, the last of which survived till 1870; and in line with these, near the eastern end of the Chapel, stood the low but picturesque buildings of the Provost's Lodge. The open space within, on which looked the Chapel and Gibbs' Building, was shaded on its eastern side by a row or grove of trees, conspicuous in many old views of Cambridge. The rest of the College, the original building, was a small quaint quadrangle north of the Chapel; it occupied precisely the site of the latest addition (1891) to the Library of the University, and from it has survived the beautiful gateway now skilfully incorporated into the Library. In this quadrangle (or, in our Cambridge parlance, this court) Simeon found his first college rooms, a set looking out on the Chapel. There he abode till he moved as a Fellow into Gibbs' Building, first into the southern rooms on the ground floor of the southern staircase, then into that set above the archway which looks through a wide semicircular window eastward towards the town. The great lawn, whose green sea stretches westward unbroken from Gibbs' Building to the river, was then crossed by a broad path leading to a now vanished bridge of two arches; and near the river, on the side towards Clare College, or, as it was called then, Clare Hall, lay the walled enclosure of the Fellows' Gardens. Beyond the river and the bridge a stately avenue of elms, of which two fragments or clumps still remain, led out to the public road. Not till 1828 did the College erect the Screen along the street-front, and the range of building which includes the Hall and the Provost's Lodge; and not till then was the Old Court sold to the University and dismantled.

Internally, as to its life of society and usage, Cambridge was no less unlike what we see now. It would be beside my purpose to attempt a detailed account of academical procedure, in which the Bachelor's degree was won by methods of examination curiously different from the present, combining tests in the main study, mathematics, with tests also in logic and divinity, and, incidentally, in Latin. It is more in point to explain that University society, under whatever influences, had sunk by Simeon's time to a discreditable level in regard both of letters and of morals.

The age of Newton and Bentley was over. Gray, of whom I
have already spoken, died at Cambridge in 1772, after forty
years of residence, and was himself both a distinguished
example of learning and refinement and the recorder of their
scarcity around him. As early as 1736 he writes to West that
'surely it was of this place, now Cambridge, but formerly
known as Babylon, that the prophet spoke when he said, "The
wild beasts of the desert shall dwell there, and their houses
shall be full of doleful creatures".' The words are a
caricature, drawn by a student who found his own classical
studies somewhat out of fashion; but the caricature affords
only a fair summary of the impression left on the reader by
the *Reminiscences* of Mr. Gunning, who entered Christ's in
1780 and died in 1854, or even by the *Recollections* of the
late Professor Pryme, who entered Trinity in 1799. The
discipline of the University had sunk in practice to the lowest
point, in spite of a formidable show or theory of authority.
The almost entirely clerical society of the 'combination-
rooms' was in many instances actually disreputable; Gunning
assures us that of the eight Seniors of Trinity about the end of
the century, there were but two or three whose character could
pass muster. In the University, as in England, a shameless
intemperance was everywhere common. Official dignity had
fallen as low as social culture; and at the great annual Fair
outside the town, Stourbridge Fair, a survival of the Middle
Ages, the populace ridiculed and insulted the Vice-Chancellor
and Proctors, who periodically degraded themselves and their
office by gluttony and intoxication, 'opening the Fair in state'.

The gloomy and unseemly picture is not without its re-
liefs. Not all colleges were alike in disorder. In 1770 died
John Cowper, fellow of Benet (now called by its ancient
name, Corpus Christi) College. His brother William, in the

Time Piece, written 1783, in a passage of severe and powerful satire, describing the then state of the Universities, pauses
and changes his tone:

> All are not such. I had a Brother once –
> Peace to the memory of a man of worth,
> A man of letters, and of manners too,
> Of manners sweet as Virtue always wears
> When gay good-nature dresses her in smiles.
> He graced a College in which order yet
> Was sacred; and was honoured, loved, and wept,
> By more than one, themselves conspicuous there.

And, no doubt, in that period of licence, personal character,
once settled aright, could develop into a strong and racy in-
dividuality better than amidst more orderly circumstances.
But when all is said for the Cambridge of the eighteenth century, the scene is still a dark one. And what is true of the
University in general, was certainly not least true of King's
College.

Religion at this unpropitious time shone feebly indeed,
alike in the University and in the town. The waves of the
great Methodist revival appear to have left Cambridge almost or quite untouched. In John Wesley's *Journal* only one
mention of the place is made, Oct. 11, 1763: 'I rode through
miserable roads to Cambridge, and thence to Lakenheath'.
On the outside of religious life little was to be seen but a
cold and soulless formalism. The churches were rarely if
ever full; the parishes were little visited by the pastors; and
in the college chapels 'the undergraduates behaved as in a
playhouse'. The churches of the neighbourhood were very
usually served, in the habitual absence of the incumbents,
by Fellows of colleges, who rode out from Cambridge on a

Sunday, and contrived by hook or crook to accomplish three
or even four 'morning services in succession'. To expedite
the process, a signal was sometimes concerted between the
parson and the clerk; the hoisting of a flag assured the rider
that there was no congregation, and that he might pass on in
peace, leaving 'Dr. Drop', so ran the phrase, 'to perform the
office'. Beneath the surface of common orthodoxy moved a
strong current of free thought, Socinian, deistic, or even athe-
istic. 'No very great wit, he believed in a God', is a significant line in Gray's *Character* of himself. John Cowper, on
his dying bed, owned to his poet-brother, his ministering angel, that the prevalent unbelief had so penetrated his life that
he had long lost all real heart for his pastoral duties at St.
Benet's Church.

Among the undergraduates, religious life, in any social
sense of that word, was unknown, as we shall see in the narrative. John Venn, Charles Simeon and a few other such men
were as a fact living at the same time in the University, and
were in earnest as Christians; but they were almost or quite
unaware of each other's existence. No 'Holy Club' of Cambridge 'Methodists' existed to draw them together and to dif-
fuse their influence.

Of the older dissenting bodies, the Baptists were the most
influential. When Simeon first knew Cambridge, their chapel
in St. Andrew's Street was a centre, if not of spiritual, certainly of some intellectual life, under the brilliant and original preaching of Robert Robinson. In 1791 a greater man
and one of the greatest of all Christian orators succeeded to
the pastorate, Robert Hall, of Bristol, Simeon's near contemporary in birth and death, and for many years his friend.

In Simeon's notices of his own early days, there occur
allusions to 'the dissenting meetings', and to the need of care

lest his own flock, once awakened to spiritual earnestness, should be scattered amongst them. It would seem that non-conformist Christians had been more zealous in Cambridge than their brethren of the Anglican Church.

Chapter 2

Cambridge – Conversion

We have seen the scholar from Eton just established in the Old Court of King's, busy there no doubt, like thousands of freshmen before him and after him, over the interests of the new life; getting his tutor's first counsels, visited by his undergraduate neighbours, and putting his rooms in order. This last work, if we may judge by his life-long love of neatness in everything about him, would be no small interest and undertaking. And thus might have begun a course of commonplace Cambridge experiences, in which the new social surroundings would be taken just as they came, and a Fellowship and perhaps a college living accepted as matters of routine, and the life lived and ended so as to leave little trace.

But three days after Simeon's arrival an incident occurred which did, in the will of God, effectually modify his whole future. In itself it was a most simple thing. The Provost, Dr. William Cooke, sent from the Lodge to tell him that within a few weeks, at mid-term, the Holy Communion was to be administered in the Chapel, and that he must communicate on that day. The message was based on a college rule now long repealed, and which perhaps never should have been enacted. As a fact it took Simeon quite by surprise. He might have met it with a passing thought of wonder, and then accepted it as inevitable; or he might have attempted a resistance, however useless. And so the mandate would have done him nothing but harm. But it was to be far otherwise; and we will hear the story in his own words, as he tells it in a private 'Memoir', written in 1813, and often to be quoted again:

> It was but the third day after my arrival that I understood I should be expected in the space of about three weeks to attend the Lord's Supper. 'What,' said I, 'must I attend?' On being informed that I must, the thought rushed into my mind that Satan himself was as fit to attend as I; and that if I must attend, I must prepare for my attendance there. Without a moment's loss of time, I bought the *Whole Duty of Man*[1], the only religious book that I had ever heard of, and began to read it with great diligence; at the same time calling my ways to remembrance, and crying to God for mercy; and so earnest was I in these exercises that within the three weeks I made myself quite ill with reading, fasting, and prayer.
>
> The first book which I got to instruct me in reference to the Lord's Supper (for I knew that on Easter Sunday I must receive it again) was Kettlewell on the Sacrament; but I remember that it required more of me than I could bear, and therefore I procured Bishop Wilson[2] on the Lord's Supper, which seemed to be more moderate in its requirements. I continued with unabated earnestness to search out and mourn over the numberless iniquities of my former life; and so greatly was my mind oppressed with the weight of them that I frequently looked upon the dogs with envy; wishing, if it were possible, that I could be blessed by their mortality, and they be cursed with my immortality in my stead. I set myself immediately to undo all my former sins, as far as I could; and did it in some instances which required great self-denial, though I do not think it quite expedient to record them; but the having done it has been a comfort to me even to this very hour, inasmuch as it gives me reason to hope that my repentance was genuine.
>
> My distress of mind continued for about three months, and well might it have continued for years, since my sins were more in number than the hairs of my head; but God in infinite condescension began

---

1. by William Law
2. Bishop of Sodor and Man from 1697-1755. His book was *A Short and Plain Instruction for the Better Understanding of the Lord's Supper*.

at last to smile upon me, and to give me a hope of acceptance with
Him.

But in Passion Week, as I was reading Bishop Wilson on the
Lord's Supper, I met with an expression to this effect – 'That the
Jews knew what they did, when they transferred their sin to the head
of their offering.' The thought came into my mind, What, may I
transfer all my guilt to another? Has God provided an Offering for
me, that I may lay my sins on His head? Then, God willing, I will not
bear them on my own soul one moment longer. Accordingly I sought
to lay my sins upon the sacred head of Jesus; and on the Wednesday
began to have a hope of mercy; on the Thursday that hope increased;
on the Friday and Saturday it became more strong; and on the Sunday morning, Easter-day, April 14, I awoke early with those words
upon my heart and lips, 'Jesus Christ is risen today! Hallelujah!
Hallelujah!' From that hour peace flowed in rich abundance into my
soul; and at the Lord's Table in our Chapel I had the sweetest access
to God through my blessed Saviour. I remember on that occasion,
there being more bread consecrated than was sufficient for the communicants, the clergyman gave some of us a piece more of it after
the service; and on my putting it into my mouth, I covered my face
with my hand and prayed. The clergyman seeing it smiled at me; but
I thought, if he had felt such a load taken off from his soul as I did,
and had been as sensible of his obligations to the Lord Jesus Christ
as I was, he would not deem my prayers and praises at all superflu-
ous.

The service in our Chapel has almost at all times been very ir-
reverently performed; but such was the state of my soul for many
months from that time that the prayers were as marrow and fatness
to me. Of course there was a great difference in my frames at different times; but for the most part they were very devout, and often,
throughout a great part of the service, I prayed unto the Lord 'with
strong crying and tears'. This is a proof to me that the deadness and
formality experienced in the worship of the Church arise far more
from the low state of our graces than from any defect in our Liturgy. If only we had our hearts deeply penitent and contrite, I know
from my experience at this hour that no prayers in the world could
be better suited to our wants or more delightful to our souls.'

Often in his correspondence does he refer to that memorable spring of 1779. 'The Passion Week,' he writes in 1807, 'I look forward to with more peculiar delight. It has always been with me a season much to be remembered, not only on account of the stupendous mysteries which we then commemorate, but because of the wormwood and the gall which my soul then tasted, twenty-eight years ago, and the gradual manifestations of God's unbounded mercy to me, till on Easterday I was enabled to see that all my sins were buried in my Redeemer's grave.'

There lies before me, as I write, the massive volume of *The Self-Interpreting Bible; with explanatory Contents, parallel Scriptures, large Notes, and practical Observations, by John Brown, Minister of the Gospel at Haddington*; printed in 1778, and bought by 'C. Simeon, King's College, Cambridge, March 24, 1785'. This Bible was his life-long companion, and is inscribed with many notes from his pen. One of these is appended to Deuteronomy 16:3: 'That thou mayest remember the day when thou camest forth out of the land of Egypt, all the days of thy life.' In the margin, in the hand of his old age, he has written thus, underlining every word: 'So must I, and God helping me so will I, the Easter Week and especially the Easter Sunday, when my deliverance was complete, in 1779.'

He does not anywhere tell us what was the passage in Bishop Thomas Wilson's book which thus carried the voice of peace and liberty to his young troubled soul. But we can scarcely doubt that it was the following:

As an Israelite, under the law, being obliged to lay his hand upon the head of his sacrifice, confessing his sins, and laying them, as it were, upon that creature – as he did easily understand that this was to show him that death was the due reward of sin; that this ought to humble him before God, and to give him the greatest abhorrence of sin, which could not be pardoned but by the loss of life of an innocent creature: – as this was plain to the meanest Israelite, even so the most unlearned Christian, when he considers that our Lord Jesus Christ became a Sacrifice for us, and that on Him all our sins were laid, on Him who knew no sin; – he will easily understand how sad our condition was which required such a Sacrifice.... He will also easily understand that the love of Christ, and the remembrance of His death, ought to be very dear to us; and that the oftener we remember it in the manner ordained, the more graces we shall receive from God, the firmer will be our faith, the surer our pardon, and the more comfortable our hopes of meeting Him, not as an enemy, but a Friend, at whose Table we have been so often entertained (Sect. II).

Such is the story of the conversion of Charles Simeon. Within a little more than two months, according to his own deliberate conviction, a conviction which only grew with time, he 'passed from death unto life', from a spiritual condition in which Jesus Christ was to him as a stranger to one in which He was everything to His servant, and so continued to be even to the end. His own record of the change, and his estimate of it, will of course be judged differently from different points of view. To some readers it may savour of egotism, to some others of exaggeration. But the frank account of a profound personal experience is not always the note of the egoist, who sometimes in his self-consciousness affects rather reserve than communication. It is not egotism that animates the spiritual confessions of a David, a Paul, an Augustine, a Luther, a Bunyan; it is the highest sort of simplicity, of naivety. It is not exaggeration necessarily which gives intensity to the picture of unregenerate self in the *Confessions*, in *Grace Abounding to the Chief of Sinners*, or in Simeon's private 'Memoir' of his early experiences. It is the intuition of a soul which has seen itself in the light of the divine holiness. And to the reader who has tasted for himself, in any degree, that indescribable but veritable experience, it will seem little necessary to inquire whether some unconfessed wickedness lay behind Simeon's account of his Eton life, or whether he is writing an empty rhapsody. 'He testifies of that he has seen' in the light of a supernatural conviction.

Let us not forget what was the region in which this profoundly awakened conscience found 'the thing called peace'. It came with the revelation to his soul of the atoning sacrifice of Jesus Christ. Bishop Wilson pointed him that way in his distress, as Evangelist pointed Christian to the shining light across the gloomy fields where he wandered with his burden; and Simeon found a light indeed. He lived long after the discovery, and always maintained an open and receptive attitude towards the whole circle of revealed truth. But where his soul first cast anchor there it held anchorage to the end. All the facts and all the mysteries of Revelation were seen by him always in relation to the central and unique truth of the atoning death of the Son of God, the glory of 'the Lamb that was slain'. Luther's 'article of a standing or falling church' was for Simeon the article of a standing or falling soul, in unalterable personal conviction.

What were the immediate results of the spiritual revolution? His own account gives a most natural and credible view of them. On the one hand he began at once to try to do good in a quiet way around him. He confided his discovery to his college friends. And as he found that his bedmaker was seldom able to go to church, he offered to 'instruct her, and any others who would join her, on Sunday evenings'; a time when worship was then unknown in the Cambridge churches. Several of the women came, and the young scholar read 'a good book' with them, and some of the prayers of the Church.

The Long Vacation arrived, and he went home, full of the same longing to impart; an instinct inseparable from a discovered joy in God. His father never gathered the household for prayers, nor did the eldest son, Richard, who lived at home. Charles had no hope that either father or brother would institute family worship at his request, so he proposed it to the servants themselves, and began. To his joy his brother cordially approved, and regularly joined the company morning and night. His father was of course aware, but never expressed either approval or displeasure.

On the other hand, the education of the young convert's Christian life was of course in an imperfect stage. It is said that he was notorious, in his freshman's year, for vanity and show in dress, and that he fairly vanquished an ambitious rival in that line, by the general verdict. And he tells us himself that in his first Long Vacation he went as usual to Reading races, and to the race-ball, 'though without the pleasure I had formerly experienced'; and that one hot Sunday in August he rode fifteen miles with a friend, an officer at Windsor, to pay a call, 'though I knew full well that I ought to keep holy the Sabbath day', and that arriving very hot and very thirsty he drank unawares to intoxication, and narrowly escaped a fatal fall on his return to Windsor. 'There have been two seasons in my life,' he writes, 'when God might have cut me off in most righteous judgment; namely in August, 1778, when my horse fell with me in Piccadilly (at which time I was in the very summit of my wickedness, without one serious concern about my soul, and when the stumbling of my horse called forth only a bitter curse at him instead of a thanksgiving to God); and on this occasion.'

Plainly, however, the man's new life in and for his God

and Redeemer 'grew exceedingly' on the whole. For three years he lived absolutely alone, as an earnest Christian, among his Cambridge coevals; not because of any pharisaic exaltation, as his whole tone of character and the manner of his narrative may assure us, but partly because his College favoured a certain isolation, and much more because such 'methodism' as he practised was almost unknown in the University. But he early grasped the secret of spiritual persistency, in a close watch upon personal habits with a view to maintaining communion with Him who sees the soul. Never was a life which at its centre was a life of pure faith lived more diligently and more watchfully at its circumference than Simeon's, in his later undergraduate time. Take a few extracts from his 'Memoir', and from his occasional scraps of Diary.

Though by nature and habit of an extravagant disposition, I practised the most rigid economy; and in this I was very much assisted by allotting my small income so as to provide for even the minutest expense, and at the same time consecrating a stated part of my income to the Lord, together with all that I could save out of the part reserved for my own use. This made economy truly delightful, and enabled me to finish my three years of scholarship without owing a shilling, whilst others, my contemporaries, incurred debts of several hundred pounds.

Saturday (Feb. 19, 1780). I began not my repentance till past twelve, and continued it all day, but exercised it chiefly on only one set of my sins, and made good resolutions concerning one, though I am wavering on the other. At Evening Chapel not so much wandering as usual.

Sunday. Prayed tolerably fervent in and before Morning Chapel, and received the Sacrament so; but after Chapel found a lassitude, and only read in Wilson till dinner: had no devotion at St. Mary's.

Had wanderings in Evening Chapel: read to servants and to Mr. R. Prayed, but very languidly, at night.

March 5th, Sunday. Morning Chapel very deficient, and much wandering. Breakfasted with Dr Glynn. Went to hear Mr. Cooke at Trinity Church, and turning at the Creed, saw the Table covered: prayed fervently, though with some wandering, and stayed the Sacrament. Mr. S. and Miss Burleigh the only two communicants – administered by Mr. Relhan. Dr. Halifax and Mr. Cooke (the preacher) went away'.

8th, Wednesday. Morning Chapel, kneeled down before service, nor do I see any impropriety in it. Why should I be afraid or ashamed of all the world seeing me do my duty? (Matthew 5:16). Ουτω λαμψατω το φος υμων.

20th, Monday (Passion Week). Morning Chapel at 10 o'clock, without surplices. When I arose, was very penitent, very devout. In Morning Chapel nearly the same. I have determined that I will neither eat nor drink all this week, except at dinner, and that sparingly, till Sunday. Evening Chapel, very fervent; at night very devout and penitent.

29th. Rose before 5, read from 6. Morning Chapel, a great deal of wandering.

June 8th. Six o'clock: after returning from the water, prayed devoutly with my servant, and am to do the same every morning and evening that I am at home. Hollis (probably his 'gyp', or manservant) will also come in the evening from this time. Morning Chapel, much earnestness and much wandering. Evening Chapel, indifferently. At night read to my servant and Hollis, and prayed with them from the Litany; and afterwards shortly by myself – very fervent.

Chapter 3

Trinity Church

Simeon was ordained Deacon, in Ely Cathedral, on Trinity Sunday, May 26, 1782. He was still under the canonical age of twenty-three, and must have obtained a faculty; a course then, but not now, possible in the matter of Deacon's orders. His 'title for Orders' was his Fellowship, to which he had succeeded January 29. The ordaining Bishop was James Yorke, a personal friend of Simeon's father; a friendship important in the sequel.

At this time he was still an undergraduate; his Bachelor's degree was not taken till January, 1783. But he had no doubt 'taken his degree in College', as the phrase was, some months already. In those days, and long afterwards, the members of King's had the singular privilege of exemption from all University examinations, as distinguished from those of their College; and the Fellowships were taken by routine and seniority. New Fellows exchanged at once the ordinary gown of the undergraduate for a more dignified robe with full sleeves.

Looking for a place of service

Though now ordained, he had no settled pastoral work in prospect, and he had been at a loss to find an incumbent under whom he could hopefully begin the labours for which he longed. Before his ordination, he tells us, he had some thoughts of putting an advertisement in the newspapers, to announce that 'a young clergyman, who felt himself an undone sinner, and who looked alone to the Lord Jesus Christ for salvation,

27

and desired to live only to make Him known, was persuaded that there must be some persons in the world whose views and feelings accorded with his own; and that if there were any minister of this description, he would gladly become his curate, and serve him gratis'.

But this singular expedient proved unnecessary. For some time before May, 1782, he had regularly attended St. Edward's Church, near King's College, a church where Hugh Latimer had ministered in his day. There he had found some spiritual assistance in the preaching of the good and loveable Vicar, Christopher Atkinson, Tutor of Trinity Hall, and gladly would have made his acquaintance, but did not care to introduce himself. He hoped that the sight of 'a young gownsman attending regularly and devoutly' would have led to an invitation. Mr. Atkinson, it afterwards appeared, had taken this undergraduate for 'a staunch Pharisee', and rather avoided him for some time. But at last the ice was broken, the invitation came, and in a conversation tete-a-tete the Vicar was greatly surprised to hear the supposed formalist 'drop some expressions which conveyed the idea of his feeling himself a poor, guilty, helpless sinner'.

Two important results followed that conversation. Mr. Atkinson introduced Simeon to John Venn of Sidney. And soon after Simeon's ordination he welcomed him as his own honorary curate.

John Venn, afterwards the beloved and honoured Rector of Clapham, was son of Henry Venn, then Rector of the secluded church of Yelling, about twelve miles west of Cambridge, just over the Huntingdonshire border. Henry Venn, Battie's University scholar in 1747, and sometime Fellow of Queens, was the descendant of a long line of clergymen, and himself as true-hearted a minister as the English Church has

ever owned. He was now a man of fifty-eight. After a laborious and singularly fruitful pastorate at Huddersfield, finding
his strength decline, he had accepted Yelling in 1771, and
there lived a life of apostolic simplicity, preaching week by
week to a congregation of shepherds and ploughmen, writing
on spiritual subjects to a large circle of correspondents, and
now latterly welcoming visits from the Cambridge friends of
his son John. If Henry Venn's conversation may be judged by
his letters, it was no wonder that these men were glad to
walk or ride over from Cambridge to the primitive village
rectory. They found there an elder friend who combined the
deepest religious experience and the purest and firmest faith
with a natural character as strong and genial as possible, and
with a great wealth of admirable good sense.[1] Simeon was
not long in making his acquaintance.

John Venn's Diary tells us the process:

> '*1782, June 1*. Drank tea at Atkinson's with Simeon, an undergradu-
> ate Fellow of King's, a religious man.'
>   '*June 2 (Sunday)*. Drank tea with Simeon (who preached his
> first sermon today at St Edwards) and Atkinson.'

On the 7th John Venn went home to Yelling, where he was
just then alone. On the 13th he writes: 'Simeon of King's
walked over from Cambridge to see me; walked on the ter-
race with him, and in church ... 14th. Rode over with Simeon
to Everton, to introduce him to Mr. Berridge[2].'

A month later, July 14, Simeon invited himself again to

---

1. Sir James Stephen (Essays in Ecclesiatical Biography, ii. 165) writes a glowing
and just eulogy on Henry Venn. One remark is strikingly true: 'There prevailed
throughout the whole man a *symphony* which enabled him to possess his soul in
order, in energy, and in composure.'
2. John Berridge was Vicar of Everton from 1755 to 1791 and was known as a
preacher of extraordinary originality and power.

Yelling, to see his friend's father: 'I propose, with the blessing of God, riding over on Tuesday morning next, before 8 o'clock, or at further a quarter after. To converse with your father has long been my desire.' He came 'and stayed till past eight at night'. No record remains of that long summer's day; but it was a bright epoch for the young curate of St. Edwards, the first day of a friendship of fourteen years which left a profound impression. Many a morning did he ride to Yelling, over the then almost hedgeless country, and in Henry Venn's holy wisdom, kind humour, and entire freedom from eccentricity, he found guidance and correctives at many critical moments in his early years of difficult ministry. His attachment to this venerable friend grew till it was a sacred passion.

To John Venn, after his father's death, he wrote thus of the sacred retrospect: 'I dislike the language of panegyric, and therefore forbear to expatiate upon a character which is, in my estimation, above all praise. Scarcely ever did I visit him, but he prayed with me. Scarcely ever did I dine with him, but his ardour in returning thanks, sometimes in an appropriate hymn, and sometimes in a thanksgiving prayer, has inflamed the souls of all present, so as to give a foretaste of Heaven itself; and in all the years that I knew him, I never remember him to have spoken unkindly of anyone, but once; and I was particularly struck with the humiliation he expressed for it, in his prayer, the next day.'

In 1833, to another of Venn's grandsons, the late Rev. John Venn, of Hereford, he writes one noble sentence of recollection: 'I wish you had known your honoured grandfather; the only end for which he lived was to make all men see the glory of God in the face of Jesus Christ.'

Henry Venn on his part has recorded some of his impressions of Simeon:

On Trinity Sunday was ordained Mr. Simeon, Fellow of King's College. Before that day he never was in company with an earnest Christian. Soon after he was visited by Mr. H. Jowsett, and my son, and two or three more. In less than seventeen Sundays, by preaching for Mr. Atkinson in a church at Cambridge, he filled it with hearers – a thing unknown there for near a century. He has been over to see me six times within the last three months: he is calculated for great usefulness, and is full of faith and love. My soul is always the better for his visits. Oh, to flame as he does with zeal, and yet be beautified with meekness! The day he was a substitute for Mr. Atkinson, he began to visit the parishioners from house to house. Full of philanthropy was his address: 'I am come to inquire after your welfare. Are you happy?' His evident regard for their good disarmed them of their bitterness; and it is amazing what success he has met with (*Life and Letters of Henry Venn*, sect. iv).

So the ministry of half a century began, in the power of spiritual sincerity and directness. The communicants were soon thrice as numerous as before. The church 'filled with hearers' must have been full indeed, to judge by one quaint story; it reaches me through the kindness of the present Vicar, the Rev. J. J. Lias, from the late Bishop Ollivant of Llandaff, who knew Simeon well. Such was the crowd which came to hear the 'substitute' that it overflowed from pews and aisles even into the sanctum of the clerk's desk. The Vicar, returning from his holiday, found his clerk perturbed, but happy in the prospect of relief; 'Oh, Sir, I am so glad you are come; now we shall have some room!' It is pleasant to think that the report of those words must almost certainly be due to the good-nature of Mr. Atkinson.

One pastoral incident of the first Sunday is preserved. Walking after service along the narrow lane near the church, St. Edward's Passage, Simeon heard through an open doorway the loud quarrelling voices of a man and his wife. Entering the house he solemnly appealed to them, and then knelt down to pray. The room was soon full of a respectful group, and the young man's reputation for loving earnestness was made already.

The summer passed in these labours. In October he was at home, watching and ministering by the death-bed of his eldest brother, Richard, 'the most affectionate of brothers', whom he saw depart in the peace of Christ. But his father and his two surviving brothers were decidedly hostile to Charles' new opinions. The father almost commanded him to renounce the friendship of their pious neighbour, the Hon. W.B. Cadogan, afterwards Vicar of St. Mary's, Reading. The brothers used every current argument to bring him out of his 'enthusiasm', but he met them, to judge from letters of this time, with equal firmness, good sense, and good temper. Both John and Edward Simeon afterwards came into full agreement with their brother. Edward died in 1813; we shall see later what his gratitude was for his younger brother's loving counsels. The father retained his prejudices to the last, and in his will left a portion to his son Charles in trust.

Yet this same son, after the eldest brother's death, had been on the point of giving up his Cambridge life and prospects that he might fill the empty place at home. It was suggested by the family that he should do so, and his only condition was that he should have a part of the house to himself, and so see his friends without interfering with his father. He was about to pack his books, and within a fortnight to vacate his new rooms in the Fellows' Building. But just then came the unlooked-for call to a very different future. Henry Therond, Minister of Trinity Church, Cambridge, died, and Simeon was appointed his successor.

Trinity Church stands in Market Street, a few paces east

of the Market Place, from which its modest spire is seen
above the houses. The tower and porch date from the thir-
teenth century, the nave from the fifteenth, and the transepts
and north aisle from the sixteenth. An ancient, low-browed
chancel, of the Decorated period, was removed in 1833, and
a new and loftier chancel built; a structure considerably re-
modelled within the last few years. Old engravings of the
interior of the church, as it was seventy years ago, show it
filled with high pews, all shut with doors. In the transept (as
now) appears a deep gallery, then reached by a staircase in
its front; but this gallery was put up by Simeon. The pulpit
(removed in 1833) was wooden, furnished with a sounding-
board; it stood just outside the chancel, to the south, and was
immediately overlooked by the transept gallery. Trinity Parish then contained about 1,500 people, resident in the streets
close to the church and in the long outlying district of King
Street, the poorer part.

'I had often,' he says in the 'Memoir' already mentioned,
'when passing Trinity Church, which stands in the heart of
Cambridge, said within myself, "How should I rejoice if God
were to give me that church, that I might preach the gospel
there and be a herald for Him in the university." But as to the
actual possession of it, I had no more prospect of attaining it
than of being exalted to the see of Canterbury.' But Therond
died, as we have seen, in that October, and Bishop Yorke
knew Mr. Simeon of Reading, and the son asked the father to
move the Bishop to appoint him. Yorke consented, apparently without hesitation, although the candidate was only a
deacon, ordained a few months before. The defect of full
orders, however, is not a legal bar to appointment to a Curacy-in-charge, and the Bishop would certainly have heard a
good character of Simeon from Atkinson of St. Edward's.

Opposition

But, although the Bishop did not hesitate, the parishioners opposed.[1] The lectureship of the seventeenth century still existed, as it still exists, and was then, as always, an institution apart from the incumbency, at least in theory. The then assistant Curate was Mr. Hammond, a name now remembered by this incident only; and the parish wanted Hammond for Minister. They resolved in any case to elect him Lecturer, and then, in a rather imperative petition, asked the Bishop of Ely to put him in charge of the parish.

It was a trying moment for Simeon, with his eager nature, his spiritual and pastoral longings, and the remarkable answer to his deepest wishes in the Bishop's consent. But he took then, as ever afterwards in the real trials of his life, a line of patience and prudence which was surely due to nothing less than secret diligence in prayer. 'I went to the vestry, and told them that I was a minister of peace; that I had no wish for the living but for the sake of doing them good; and that I would, if upon further reflection it did not appear to be improper, write to the Bishop to say that I declined any further competition.' He did so, but the letter missed the post; and then he felt himself entitled, by the reserve with which he had spoken, to withhold it, and passively to await the Bishop's answer to the petition. If he were appointed, he would make Hammond his 'substitute' and give him all the profits of the benefice.

But the parishioners were not so deliberate, or so generous. As soon as Simeon had left the vestry, they sent to Ely to

---

1. This Lecture was an institution expressly sanctioned by the King in Council, and was sustained by subscriptions gathered from all the parishes in the town. An entry in the parish register for November, 1610, shows that it was already in existence then.

announce that he had retired, and to press their candidate again. Bishop Yorke, however, was not to be thus coerced out of his choice, and in a letter which still exists, yellow with time, he told Simeon that the church was his, if he would accept it. 'From respect to your father (who has wrote in your favour) and confidence in your character, I had intended to have entrusted this preferment to your care. The parishioners have petitioned for Mr. Hammond, and unless gratified insinuate their intentions of bestowing their Lectureship on another person than my Curate. I do not like that mode of application, and, if you do not accept it, shall certainly not license Mr. Hammond. I shall await your answer.'

The knot was thus cut. To decline the church would not give it to Hammond, and to make him the 'substitute of the Minister' would now seem a slight upon the Bishop. Simeon accepted the charge, and preached his first sermon in Trinity Church on November 10, 1782, the day after the Bishop wrote the decisive letter.

I need not explain how very unpopular the appointment was; it was very plainly shown to be so. The parishioners chose Hammond Lecturer at once. By the usage of the office he thus had a right to the pulpit every Sunday afternoon, leaving only the morning to Simeon. That right he exercised for five years, and was then followed for seven years by another clergyman, equally independent. Not till 1794 was the Minister chosen to be Lecturer also. And on Sunday mornings the church for a long while was made as inaccessible as possible to him and his hearers. The pew doors were almost all locked, and the should-be occupants were absent, leaving only the aisles for any congregation that might assemble. On the first Sunday aisles and pews alike were nearly empty when the service began, a bitter trial for the lately popular young clergyman; but after a while people trooped in; and 'multitudes', as the weeks went on, were unable to find room. Simeon set forms in the aisles, and even put up open seats in nooks and corners at his own expense; but these the church-wardens pulled down and threw into the churchyard.

To visit his people at their homes was impossible of course for the present; scarcely a door would open to Charles Simeon. 'In this state of things I saw no remedy but faith and patience. The passage of Scripture which subdued and controlled my mind was this, "The servant of the Lord must not strive". It was painful indeed to see the church, with the exception of the aisles, almost forsaken; but I thought that if God would only give a double blessing to the congregation that did attend, there would on the whole be as much good done as if the congregation were doubled and the blessing limited to only half the amount. This comforted me many, many times, when, without such a reflection, I should have sunk under my burden.

'I wished rather to suffer than to act; because in suffering I could not fail to be right; but in acting I might easily do amiss. Besides, if I suffered with a becoming spirit, my enemies, though unwittingly, must of necessity do me good; whereas if in acting I should have my own spirit unduly exercised, I must of necessity be injured in my own soul, however right-eous my cause might be.'

Chapter 4

The Parish

Simeon's appointment was welcome news to his growing circle of godly friends, younger and older. Through Henry Venn of Yelling he had already become known to that illustrious Christian layman, John Thornton (1720–1790), Venn's early friend, and the friend and active helper of John Newton and Thomas Scott, and indeed of a host of good men and good causes. 'He was,' says Sir James Stephen in his Essays, 'one of those rare men in whom the desire to relieve distress assumes the form of a master-passion' (ii. 292). Cowper wrote a noble elegy on his death:

> Thou hadst an industry in doing good,
> Restless as his who toils and sweats for food.
> Avarice in thee was the desire of wealth
> By rust imperishable, or by stealth;
> And if the genuine worth of gold depend
> On application to its noblest end,
> Thine had a value in the scales of heaven,
> Surpassing all that mine or mint had given.

But I must not yield to the temptation to speak at length of Thornton, merchant-prince, saint, wise counsellor, unwearied giver and worker in the cause of God and man. He touches Simeon's life, so far as I know, at very few points only; but it was an important touch which he gave now, in a letter of manly Christian counsel, sent at once on hearing of his young friend's new charge at Cambridge. Let me quote the letter from the manuscript just as it is written:

Clapham, 13th November 1782

Dear Sir,

I was glad to hear the Books came so timely, and that the Bishop of Ely had sent you the presentation to Trinity Church; may a gracious God guide, direct and bless all your Ministrations, to the Redeemer's glory, and make you a blessing to many.

Permit me to use an uncommon freedom, and I hope you'll forgive me should you not be able to join issue in Sentiment with me. What I would recommend is to set off with only the usual Service that has been performed, as by that means I apprehend you'll gain upon the people gradually, and you can at any time increase your duty as you see occasion, and I should on the same principle advise against exhorting from House to House as heretofore you did. I assure you a subtil Adversary as often obtains his end by driving too fast as too slow, and perhaps with religious people oftener.

Remember it is God who works and not you, and therefore if you run before the pillar and the cloud you will assuredly be bewildered.

The Lord ever was and ever will be with the small still voice, and therefore beware of noisy professors; they are far more to be dreaded than the Worldly-minded.

Watch continually over your own spirit, and do all in love; we must grow downwards in humility to soar Heavenward.

I should recommend your having a watchful eye over yourself, for generally speaking as is the Minister so are the people. If the Minister is enlightened, lively and vigorous, his Word will come with power upon many and make them so; if he is formal the infection will spread among his hearers; if he is lifeless, spiritual death will be visible thro the greatest part of the Congregation; therefore if you watch over your own soul you may depend upon it your people will keep pace with you generally, or at least that is the way to the blessing.

It is a sad tho' too common a mistake to be more regardful of others than ourselves, and we must begin at home; many regard watchfully the outward work and disregard that within.

Your Sermons should be written, well digested and becoming a Scholar, not over long but pithy, that those who seek occasion may find none except in the matter of your God.

May the God of all Grace grant unto us and all that are dear to us
the repentance of Peter, the faith of Paul, and the love of John, and
be with you at all times and in all places, and with

Dear Sir,
Your affectionate Friend
and hearty wellwisher,
John Thornton.

The Rev Mr. Simeon.

Letter from John Newton

Ten days later another and longer letter reached him, dated
'Hoxton, London'. It was from John Newton (1725-1807), of
old the godless sailor-lad, then the captain of a slave-ship on
the Atlantic; later, after long convictions, in which a glance
at Thomas à Kempis had a place, brought under Whitefield's
mighty influence; at length ordained; Curate-in-charge of
Olney for fifteen years, and now recently made Rector of St.
Mary Woolnoth in the City. Newton's repute for Christian
good sense had already led Simeon to his door in Charles
Square, Hoxton; and he now wrote a letter of admirable counsel, spiritual and practical, to his Cambridge friend. A few
sentences must be the sample:

The Lord sees fit to fix you in a noble stand indeed. Were I a colle-
gian, I think I should prefer a church in one of our Universities (and
perhaps Cambridge especially) to any station in the kingdom. And
yet I overrate myself in thinking I would dare to make such a choice,
were it in my power.... He has chosen for you, and on Him therefore
you may confidently rely for all that patience, fortitude, and meekness of wisdom which you will need, especially in a place where so
many eyes will be upon you, so many tongues ready to circulate
every report to your prejudice, and so many ears open to receive
them.

Your sense of His great goodness, and the strong impression you have received of the power and reality of unseen things, have inspired you with a commendable zeal. Shall I advise you to repress your zeal? Far from it. It would better become me to wish to catch fire from you than to attempt to chill you by the cold maxims which often pass for prudence. Yet there is such a thing as true Christian prudence, and perhaps at this time Satan may not attempt to damp your zeal, but to push you to extremes, to make you throw unnecessary difficulties in your own way, and thereby to preclude your usefulness. If the heart be right with God, the best means for avoiding this overdoing is a close attention to the *whole* Scripture. Detached texts or sentences may seem to countenance what by no means will accord with the general tenor of the *whole*. Particularly the spirit and conduct of our Lord in the days of His humiliation furnish the best model. His manner, His gentleness, His patient attention to the weakness and prejudices of those around Him, we cannot imitate too closely.

But then the man is to beware on the other side:

I have known more ministers than one greatly hurt when they have been able to smile upon the well-meant indiscretions they committed when their experience was but small. By degrees zeal instead of being regulated is extinguished, till at length the love of the world and the fear of man prevail. Thus I have seen some frozen into mere lifeless images of their former selves, and some have not even retained a resemblance of what they were. So I have almost by habit a fear and jealousy over those who are remarkably warm and active at their first setting out.

'I have left little room for an apology if necessary. But I hope you will not expect one. I love you and wish you well, and shall be glad to hear from you whenever you are at leisure.

Believe me to be, dear Sir,
Your affectionate friend and servant,
John Newton.

Letter from Henry Venn
Let me add here, though it belongs to a rather later time, a
scrap from a letter of Henry Venn's:

> Yelling, August 6th, 1784.
> My Dear Friend,
> Were my advice to be taken, I would rather have you give place to
> the rising prejudice against your preaching than to oppose it and
> preach in spite of them. Be not afraid of them. Your meek submis-
> sion will be of more service than any preaching, for it will convince
> the spectator of your conduct that you are not high-minded, and
> overfond of hearing yourself, or important in your own eyes, as if
> the work of the Lord could be carried on by no body but yourself,
> which is their present false judgment.
>
>   From your affectionate and obliged friend,
>   H. Venn.
> '*Above all* things have fervent charity among yourselves.'

A little earlier the same 'obliged friend', himself as brave
as he was wise, had written to Simeon (December 20, 1783):
'Thou art called to be a man of war from thy youth. May the
Captain of our salvation be thy guide, shield, and strength.'
These extracts throw a suggestive light on both Simeon's
character and his circumstances. Evidently his elder friends
did not think for a moment that he would fail in courage or
energy; they feared for his moderation and discretion. We
have already seen how well he had begun with his new parishioners even in this respect, and the development of practical and balanced wisdom as he goes on is remarkable. But
the fire of those first days evidently sometimes threatened
conflagration, as his strong spirit was affronted not so much
by personal insults as by contempt of his work and message.
Henry Venn's daughter, Mrs. Elliott, used to tell a story which
shows us Simeon at that time, under a side-light, ready to

reveal even at Yelling a certain harshness and self-assertion. He had just ridden away after a visit at the rectory, and first one Miss Venn and then another exclaimed about his manner. 'Come into the garden, children,' their father said, and led them out into that favourite schoolroom. 'Now, pick me one of those peaches.' But it was early summer, and the time for peaches was not yet; how could their father ask for the green fruit? 'Well, my dears, it is green now, and we must wait; but a little more sun, and a few more showers, and the peach will be ripe and sweet. So it is with Mr. Simeon.'

Opposition continues

The belligerents in Trinity parish, however, were in a mood to attack the most good-natured man who was not the man of their choice. Long and painful was the siege laid against Simeon's activity and influence. After many months of waiting he began a Sunday evening lecture, that is a six o'clock service followed by an unwritten exposition; an almost unprecedented innovation. It was at once largely attended. But after the first few Sundays the uncompromising churchwardens shut the church doors, and carried off the keys, while the people stood waiting in the street. For that one time Simeon had the doors opened by a smith, but he thought it wiser to drop the enterprise for the present. 'Their behaviour,' he writes to John Venn, 'has been highly displeasing to the whole parish, except two or three enemies of the gospel. Nor has it been less illegal than uncivil. May God bless them with enlightening grace. I shall renew the lecture next summer.'

But he did not realise the hope so soon. The 'illegal' opposition continued, at intervals, for nearly ten years; and in March, 1792, he stated the case for an opinion to Sir William Scott, afterwards Lord Stowell; and case and opinion

lie in manuscript before me. It appears that the evening lecture was begun mainly in the interest of the servants of the
colleges, and that the wardens claimed the right to stay it
because 'the church was not a vicarage'. The opinion was
decisively for 'the sequestrator', provided he had the approval of 'the Bishop, whose Curate he is'. At the same time
an opinion was obtained which asserted the illegality of lock-
ing ordinary church-pews. But I do not find that Simeon 'took
the law' against his opponents, though he had thus carefully
ascertained it; a piece of practical wisdom fruitful for the
future.

All this while he was both diligently preaching to his aisle-
congregations and doing his utmost to organize his pastoral
work. Among his manuscripts is a sermon dated April, 1783,
intended plainly to be a deliberate statement (it is a deeply
heart-searching one) of his view of the calling and responsi-
bilities of a clergyman. I find not the slightest allusion to
parochial troubles; all is aimed at the Minister himself; the
people are desired, in a tone of manly freedom, to weigh his
conduct and his words as those who are entitled to watch
him, but also bound to pray for him. Thus he closes:

> It may be asked, perhaps, Why do you speak to us about the duties
> of the Ministry, when we come to hear concerning our own duties?
> I have done it for your sakes as well as for my own – for your sakes,
> because by remembering the very nature of my office, and the care
> incumbent on me for the welfare of your immortal souls, you will
> consider whatever may appear in my discourses harsh, earnest or
> alarming, not as the effects of enthusiasm, but as the rational dic-
> tates of a heart impressed with a sense both of the value of the soul
> and the importance of eternity; and by recollecting the awful con-
> sequences of my neglect, you will be more inclined to receive fa-
> vourably any well-meant admonitions. I have spoken also on this
> subject for my own sake, that I may be stirred up to reading, medita-

tion and prayer, and the performance of all my ministerial duties. But as my most solemn engagements and actual purposes at present, like the zealous protestations of Peter, will soon be forgotten and falsified if I am still left to my own deceitful and corrupt heart, let me beseech you, in St. Paul's words, to 'pray for me, and for all' ministers, that we may be replenished with the truth of the Gospel, and enabled to declare the whole counsel of God, so that the ignorant may be instructed, the wavering confirmed, the feeble comforted, and the strong established, and that both we who sow in preaching God's Word, and you who reap in hearing it, may rejoice together for ever and ever.

Such a style of address, grave and candid, and totally free from that easy but fatal mistake of troubled pastors, the scolding accent, gave a favourable omen for the future of this man, not yet twenty-four years old. And his labours in the pulpit were supported the while by more private efforts. General visitation from house to house was, as we have seen, impossible, but many of his flock began to show themselves moved to his message and to seek more private intercourse with him; and he on his part saw their need of more methodical teaching, if they were not to drift. His own 'Memoir' shall take up the story:

What was to be done? If those whose minds were impressed by my preaching had not some opportunity of further instruction, they would infallibly go to the dissenting meetings, and thus be gradually drawn away from the Church. The only alternative I had was to make them meet in a private room; I therefore hired a small room in my parish, and met them there, and expounded to them the Scripture, and prayed with them. In time the room was too small to hold us all, and I could not get one larger in my parish; I therefore got one in an adjoining parish, which had the advantage of being very spacious and very retired. Here I met my people for a considerable time. I was sensible that it would be regarded by many as irregular; but what was to be done? I could not instruct them in my church; and

I must of necessity have them all drawn away by the dissenters, if I did not meet them myself; I therefore committed the matter to God in earnest prayer, and entreated Him that, if it were His will that I should continue the room, He would graciously screen me from persecution on account of it; or that if persecution should arise on account of it, He would not impute it to me as sin if I gave up the room. He knew the real desire of my heart; He knew that I only wished to fulfil His will: I told Him a thousand times over that I did not deprecate persecution; for I considered that as the necessary lot of all who would 'live godly in Christ Jesus', and more especially of all who would preach Christ with fidelity; but I deprecated it as arising from that room.

'The "room" was certainly irregular, for the assembly was extra-parochial and might even have been regarded in law as a forbidden conventicle. But its purpose was wholly in favour of order and co-hesion, and as a fact no mischief followed. During the space of many years no persecution whatever arose from that room, though con-fessedly it was the side on which my enemies might have attacked me with most effect.'

Sub-dividing of hearers into groups

Allusions to the work done in this gathering occur often in Simeon's pastoral annals. It was the occasion of all others when he could deal hand to hand with the spiritual state of individuals. As his acceptance in the parish grew so did the 'Society', and after a while it came to be so large that it was broken up into six. These sub-societies, classed with care according to sex, age, and other conditions, each met the Min-ister once in a month. Alms for the poor were collected at each meeting, and the leaders, regularly designated, were the Minister's stewards for the distribution. This parochial or-ganisation had its grave drawbacks, at a time when ill-health made it hard for Simeon to keep his hand as firmly as usual on the working; some of the stewards betrayed a deplorable self-assertion and disloyalty, and were at last reluctantly shut out. But Simeon, after thirty years, was deliberately of opinion that some such methods were necessary, if a pastor was to keep his flock together.

> After all this experience, What is my judgement in relation to private Societies? My judgment most decidedly is that without them, where they can be had, a people will never be kept together; nor will they ever feel related to their minister as children to a parent; nor will the minister himself take that lively interest in their welfare which is both his duty and his happiness to feel. A minister is to be 'instant in season and out of season'; and if his public labours are comprehended under the former period, these private exercises seem especially intended by the latter: and one who would approve himself to God, as St. Paul did, should be able to say, 'I have taught you publicly, and from house to house, and have warned you night and day with tears.' But then great care should be taken about the manner of conducting them. The people should never, if it can be avoided, be left to themselves; the moment they are, there is danger of an unhallowed kind of emulation rising up among them; and those who by reason of their natural forwardness are most unfit to lead, will always obtrude themselves as leaders among them, whilst the modest and timid will be discouraged, because they cannot exercise those gifts which they behold in others. On such occasions too the vain and conceited will be peculiarly gratified; and, mistaking the gratifications of vanity for truly spiritual emotions, they will attach a pre-eminent importance to those opportunities which tend to display their talents.... This therefore a minister must guard against with all his might; and if he makes it a rule to conduct the service in the private societies himself, he will, for the most part, keep down these evils. It was not till I was laid aside by my long indisposition, that these evils showed themselves in any considerable degree; and after all, if we will not establish such societies for fear of such consequences, we must remember that there is a Charybdis as well as a Scylla, and that in all human institutions we have only as it were a choice of evils, there being nothing perfect under the sun.

Some view of his estimate of the true pastor's function, and some details also of his own methods, may be got from a letter written in his old age (1829) to Bishop Summer of Winchester:

> I have seen, my Lord, of very recent date a little pamphlet, wherein a Minister is set forth in Herbert's way as the father, the physician, etc, etc, of his parish; but my judgment did not go along with it. In a very small parish these duties may be combined; but it appears to me that, comparatively, this is serving tables. A pastor has other and higher duties to attend to. His wife (if he have one) should be the mother of the parish; but he must not, so to speak, be the father; he must be the pastor. The giving himself to the Word of God and prayer seems to me to be his peculiar duty; and the paternal part (of administering relief, etc.) should, I think, be delegated to others under his superintendence, as Moses delegated many of his duties to the seventy employed by him. This is what I have done myself for nearly fifty years; I have thirty (male and female) in their different districts, and I preach an annual Sermon in aid of their efforts. By these, I hope, great good has been done; whilst by their supplying my lack of service, I have been left at liberty to follow that line of duty which was more appropriate to my own powers, and which I could not have prosecuted if I had not thus contrived to save my time.

This chapter shall close with one extract more from Henry Venn, writing to his son-in-law, Charles Elliott, of Brighton:

> January 8, 1790.
> On Monday my affectionate friend Simeon walked over and slept here. Oh, how refreshing were his prayers, how profitable his conversation! We were all revived; he left a blessing behind him... He preaches twice a week in a large room. My daughter attended there when I preached; and his people are indeed of an excellent spirit – merciful, loving, and righteous.

Chapter 5

The University

It is time to turn from Simeon's parochial labours to the beginnings of his work and influence in the University, through
which he moved so powerfully the life of the English Church
and of Christians far beyond our borders.

He took an active part for many years in the administra-
tive duties of his College. He long held one or other of the
Deanships at King's (there were then three); 1788 to 1790,
1792 to 1798, 1827 to 1830. He was Second Bursar from
1798 to 1805, and Vice-Provost (young as he was) from 1790
to 1792.

Both as Dean and as Vice-Provost he strove to do his duty.
When he became Dean of Divinity, in 1789, his early friend
Thomas Lloyd wrote to him:

> I congratulate you on your appointment, and on the very good dis-
> position of the Provost towards you. This you are to consider a new
> talent, of no small importance. O use it faithfully, and remember
> you are as much accountable for the improvement of it as for the
> discharge of your parochial duty. Lay yourself out for usefulness
> no less in the University than in the town. Your influence in your
> own College is evidently increasing; nay, further, the Provost is in-
> clined to co-operate with you in reforming the College. Try then
> how far he will proceed with you; yet try judiciously. Give the present
> state of our College and of the University at large its proper pro-
> portion of your attention and your prayers.

Henry Venn, in a letter written March, 1791, mentions a
night's visit to Yelling from 'dear Simeon, now Mr Vice-

Provost'. In this office he was called upon at once to use his authority in a painful case of discipline, summarily excluding from residence a Fellow, his senior, who had been 'sent away for scandalous behaviour, and had reappeared during the Long Vacation, while the Provost was absent, as shameless as ever'. Dr. Glynn was Simeon's helper in this difficult action, and Provost Cooke, answering Simeon's report, wrote that 'yourself and Dr. Glynn will ever have my hearty thanks for your prudent and spirited conduct'.

While thus active in his College, he had already begun to make himself felt as a teacher and guide among the undergraduates in general. I find no express account of the first steps to this; nor was it likely. In Simeon's case, as in that of many men who have exercised a wide religious influence, the influence was not contrived; it came. No doubt he had longed in his early days to have Trinity Church, that he might there 'preach the Gospel in the University'. But the wish was as simple as possible in its scope. It was long before he dreamed of being 'a leader of religion', and never did he *affect* that character when leadership was actually laid on him by circumstances.

It was certain, however, that when once he became Minister of Trinity, the church would be frequented by undergraduates, for good or ill. He was a Fellow of King's; he had already made a name for powerful preaching at St. Edward's; and he was reported to be at war with his parishioners. Trinity Church was literally locked, as far as possible, against its Minister, and the Minister was resolutely reading prayers and preaching before a congregation gathered in the aisles. Here was quite enough to draw undergraduates in a crowd at first. And when they had once come, they found a man whose sermons, both by substance and manner, attracted at least their

curiosity, and soon either greatly benefited them, as a divine
message reached the soul, or by a fearless freedom challenged their contradiction and opposition.

I shall speak later in detail of Simeon's theology, and of
his characteristics as a preacher. Here it is enough to say that
he possessed some really great gifts both of utterance and
action, and that, in an age when preaching was too often
defaced by either a studied monotony of delivery or great
affectation, he avoided both evils. Perfect naturalness and
the utmost life and energy marked his manner.

His matter was never trivial, and he never for a moment
wandered into idle rhetoric. To expound the Scripture before him as closely and clearly as he could, and then to bring
its message to bear full on the conscience and will of the
hearers, was his settled aim from the first kept in view intel-
ligently and with great pains. And what was his doctrine? In
two words, it was Jesus Christ. Everything in Simeon's
preaching radiated from Jesus Christ, and returned upon Him.
Not that he forced texts away from their surroundings, and
forgot the literal in the mystical. But he was sure that Christ
is the burden of the words of the Prophets and the Apostles;
and he knew that He was everything for Charles Simeon.

Mere moral essays in the pulpit were for him impossible,
though no man could well hold the standard of virtue and
duty higher than he did. And so were merely critical discussions, though he always stimulated his hearers to think. For
him Christ was the centre of all subjects for sinful man; and
all his hearers were for him sinful men, for whom the Gospel
was the one remedy. Christ was the Gospel; and personal
faith in Him, a living Person, was the Gospel secret. To Christ
all men were called, for 'pardon, and holiness, and heaven;
and those who came at that call belonged thenceforth to Christ,

His property, bound to live and die to their Lord'. Simeon himself thus describes the three great aims of all his preaching: 'To humble the sinner, To exalt the Saviour, To promote holiness'.

Such was the heart and soul of his message. Whatever else he taught, all was gathered round these two *foci*, the sin of man and the glory of the Redeemer. No one, I say it confidently, ever preached a soberer Gospel from that great primeval text; no one was ever more free than Simeon's writings show him to have been from unpractical rhapsodies, from fanciful appendages to his main message. He was a true man himself, and he was deeply in earnest that others should be true.

Nor was he forgetful of the actual conditions of human life. The plain duties of the hour and day, however secular on their surface, were sacred things in his eyes. Social intercourse, physical recreation, intellectual labour and delight, were never in his teaching laid under the censure of a mistaken asceticism. The courtesies of life were always honoured in his own practice; the friends of his later years admired in him a fine example of the old politeness. The claims of the Church and of the State on the Christian's loyalty and service were his frequent theme when he came to apply truth to life; and so were the claims of the University and the College.

His whole influence over his undergraduate followers went persistently in the direction of their doing first the duties which they came to Cambridge to do. But then everything was viewed 'no longer after the flesh', but always in relation to the sin of man and to the royal rights of Christ. The preacher's sober reasoning and living eloquence all meant that man must come out of himself to his Redeemer, and surrender to

Him, giving over into His hands without reserve the soul, the life, the day. This was made unmistakably clear, whatever might be the collision with common notions of religion and a popular standard of morals.

In this fearless delivery of an uncompromising spiritual message I read almost the whole account of Simeon's early experiences of persecution and reproach in his University. No doubt there were other minor causes. The circumstances of his appointment to Trinity Church not only alienated many of his parishioners, but were sure to prompt them (for they were human) to speak evil of him to the students who came to listen. From the very first, and for many years after, he was personally slandered as a bad man who had a high profession of goodness; a terrible dagger-thrust at any time, but never more so than when, as then, the outward practice of religion has fallen into general neglect. But the evidence shows that in Simeon's case, if ever in any man's, the great burden to be borne was 'the offence of the Cross'. He preached a message as old as the Apostles and their Master, but long forgotten in those days in the average life of the University. Its relative novelty gave point to its soul-searching demands; and the human heart rebelled.

Certainly little advantage in the way of support from the leaders of the University was with Simeon at first. A few men of influence were in essential agreement with him; particularly Isaac Milner of Queens and William Farish of Magdalene. Milner, Senior Wrangler of 1774 (Incomparabilis was added to his name in the list), was chosen President of Queens in 1788, and long exercised strong, if sometimes rough, personal authority in University life. Farish, the Senior Wrangler of 1778, gentlest of men but having a noble courage of convictions, was an able scientific student, and became

Jacksonian Professor in 1813[1]. Almost from the first he was Simeon's firm and helpful friend; and with him may be reckoned Atkinson, and Coulthurst, Fellow of Sidney. But they were almost alone of their order for some time. And Milner, with a totally different character from Simeon's, sent to college by his elder brother Joseph from the loom at Leeds, shrewd and rugged, a keen observer, at first stood in doubt of the new Etonian preacher, and cared to watch rather than support. In time, however, he entirely trusted him, and was his resolute helper. I find him in 1794, 'preaching to a serious congregation at Simeon's church in the morning, and hearing him preach a faithful discourse in the evening'.

As a rule the Heads of Houses and other chief men looked unfavourably upon Simeon, and made their dislike and suspicions felt in many ways very trying to him and those who attached themselves to him. In one college, for instance, a regular Greek Testament lecture was begun on Sunday nights, with the well-understood purpose of preventing attendance at Simeon's evening service. He met this difficulty in the wisest way when his undergraduate friends told him of it; he advised them to set a careful example of regular attendance and attention, letting it be seen that 'methodism' did not mean neglect of duty. After a few years the lecture was given up, on the protest of one of the Fellows of the college.

Long after the first days of trial the undergraduate who worshipped at Simeon's church ran some academical risks,

1. One of his old pupils, the late Rev. John Venn of Hereford told me (in 1886) that Farish was examined before an early Parliamentary Committee on Railways. He gave is as his opinion that steam carriages might run at 60 miles per hour, though 30 miles would be a better common pace. He was questioned no further; and he heard afterwards that the Committee were unanimous in a private verdict of an *unsound mind!*

so strong was the suspicion against his principles. In one case, related to me by the man most concerned (a dignitary of the Church in his later days), a great injustice was done; an act which would be utterly impossible now and which may seem almost incredible as it was. A candidate for a college prize found himself at the foot of the list, but learnt afterwards (by the examiner's inadvertence) that his marks had actually put him at the head. The marks were cancelled by notorious and obstinate Simeonism. This, however, was an instance by itself; the general opposition was more honest in its methods.

In all this we have little more than particular instances of the trials to which almost everywhere for many years the best of the clergy called Evangelicals (or to use the older term, Methodists) were called to submit. Many a curious tradition lives – with no bitterness in its life – among the descendants of those men. The late Rev. Henry Venn, for thirty years Secretary of the Church Missionary Society, the son of Simeon's friend John Venn, records what follows from his own experience:

> In the present day it will hardly be credited; but one of these early recollections (of about 1808) may serve as a specimen.... A near relative of the Bishop of London, after being a guest at Fulham Palace, was to visit Mr. (John) Venn at Clapham. We (the two sons) were ourselves sent to wait at the Bull's Head, a mere public house, three hundred yards from the Rectory at Clapham, and to bring the visitor to the Rectory. The truth being that the Bishop of London could not allow his carriage to be seen to draw up at Mr. Venn's Rectory, though it might be seen to set down a lady at a small public house.

Dealing with disturbances in his church
But I return to Cambridge, and to Simeon's early preachings in Trinity Church, as they reached University men, and to the animosity they roused. From his own retrospect, the 'Memoir' already quoted, I take the following passages. The first refers to a time when he had at last succeeded in introducing an evening service:

At first, and indeed for several years, the keeping of order in my church was attended with considerable difficulty. The novelty of an evening service in a parish church in Cambridge attracted some attention. In the college chapels it was no novelty; but in a parish church it conveyed at once the impression that it must be established for the advancement of true religion, or what the world would call Methodism. Hence it is not to be wondered at that it should be regarded with jealousy by some and with contempt by others; or that young gownsmen, who even in their own chapels show little more reverence for God than they would in a playhouse, should often enter in to disturb our worship.

I appointed persons to stand with wands in all the aisles; and as the chief disturbance was generally made when the congregation was leaving the church, I always went down from my pulpit the moment the service was finished, and stood at the great north door, ready to apprehend any gownsman who should insult those who had been at church. I endeavoured always to act with mildness but yet with firmness, and through the goodness of God was enabled to keep in awe every opposer. I requested those who withstood my authority not to compel me to demand their names, because, if once constrained to do that, I must proceed to further measures. This kindness usually prevailed. Where it did not, I required the person to call upon me the next morning; nor did ever one single instance occur of a person daring to refuse my mandate. On several occasions stones were thrown in at the windows, and the offenders escaped, but in one instance a young man, the very minute after he had broken a window, came in. I charged the act upon him; upon which, conceiving himself detected, he acknowledged the truth of the allegation. About this time the disturbances had risen to such a height that it was necessary I should make an example. I therefore laid the matter before the Vice-Chancellor; who, far beyond my most sanguine expectations, acknowledged the enormity of the offence, and offered to proceed with the culprit in any way I should require. I did not wish to hurt the young man; but it was indispensably necessary that I should act in a way that should intimidate all the men in the University. Unless they should be reduced to order, I must entirely lay aside my lectures, both on Sunday and Thursday evenings; but as such a sacrifice would be most injurious to the cause of God in the whole town, I determined either, as we say, to kill or cure. I required that the offender should read, in the midst of the congregation, a public acknowledgement written by myself; and this the young man did on the following Sunday evening, begging pardon of the congregation for having disturbed them, and thanking me for my lenity in not having proceeded against him with the rigour which his offence deserved. The church was very full of gownsmen, and the young man, in the most conspicuous place in the church, read the acknowledgement immediately after the prayers; and because he, as might have been expected, did not read it so that all the congregation might distinctly hear it, I ordered him to deliver me the paper, and then myself read it in the most audible manner before them all.[1]

During this time the utmost curiosity prevailed; all standing up upon the forms and seats, but there was at the same time an awe upon all; and I then went up into the pulpit, and preached from those words, Galatians 4:7,8: 'Be not deceived; God is not mocked; whatsoever a man soweth, that shall he also reap', etc. My sermon was heard with the deepest attention, and for a long time my enemies were all subdued before me. I have sometimes doubted whether I

---

1. The paper which was thus read (November 16, 1794) still exists. It begins: 'I ...., of .... College, sensible of the great offence I have committed in disturbing this congregation on Thursday last, do, by the express order of the Vice-Chancellor, thus publicly beg pardon of the Minister and congregation, &.' Simeon's introductory comments are also preserved, carefully written out. In the course of them he says: 'We have seen persons coming into this place in a state of intoxication; we have seen them walking about the aisles; we have seen them insulting persons both in and after divine service; in short the devotions of the congregation have been disturbed by every species of misconduct .... I have been averse to make an example; nor is it without the greatest reluctance that I now call forth a young man of liberal education to make a public acknowledgement.'

was not guilty of undue severity in reading the paper a second time myself; but when I consider the extremity to which I was reduced, I am disposed to think that I did right.

There was one particular instance, in which a degree of severity on my part was attended with the happiest effects. Two young men, now blessed servants of the Most High God, came into my church in a most disorderly way; and, as usual, I fixed my eyes upon them with sternness. One of them was abashed; but the other, the only one that ever was daring enough to withstand my eye, looked at me again with undaunted, not to say with impious, confidence, refusing to be ashamed. I sent for him the next morning, and represented to him the extreme impiety of his conduct, contrasting it with those who were less hardened; and warning him, Who it was that he thus daringly defied ('He that despiseth you, despiseth Me; and he that despiseth Me, despiseth Him that sent Me'); and I enjoined him never to come into that church again, unless he came in a very different spirit. To my surprise I saw him there again the following Sunday, but with a more modest countenance; and from that time he continued to come, till it pleased God to open his eyes and to lead him into the full knowledge of the Gospel of Christ, and in a year or two afterwards he became a preacher of that faith which once he had despised.

The man thus changed was for many years, till his death in 1833, one of Simeon's inmost circle of friends. He was John Sargent, the biographer of Henry Martyn. He was to have written the 'Memoir' of Simeon himself had he survived him. 'I had desired my most beloved friend, Mr. Sargent,' he writes to Mr. Carus, 'to undertake the work, if it *must* be undertaken.' But Sargent died just as he was about to visit Simeon and receive the materials from his hands. He left a memory singularly dear and beautiful behind him.

In that book of much curious and often sorrowful interest to readers of academic history, Gunning's *Reminiscences*, the author, a most impartial observer, who well remembered Simeon's early days, writes about these troubles:

For many years (I speak from my own personal knowledge) Trinity
Church and the streets leading to it were the scenes of the most
disgraceful tumults. In vain did Simeon, with the assistance of persons furnished with white wands, exert himself to preserve order in
the church; in vain did Professor Farish, who as Moderator was well
known and popular with the undergraduates, for some years before
and after he was Proctor, station himself at the outside door to prevent improper conduct to the persons leaving the church; and though
one undergraduate, who had been apprehended by Simeon, was compelled to read a public apology in the church, the disturbances continued.

Gunning's account and Simeon's own supplement each other.
Comparatively, the strong measures taken did make a great
change for the better, but the better was still very far from
what it should be. And Gunning's description of the general
wild licence of word and behaviour among the undergraduates of those days makes it less remarkable that in the particular case of Trinity Church they should have acted as they
did.

On one occasion in that early time a party of these men
determined to assault Simeon personally as he left the church
after service. They assembled at the chief entrance, the north
door in Market Street, in such numbers that it would have
been difficult to disperse them before some cruel violence
had been inflicted; and Simeon had always left the church by
the north door on his way back to King's. But that Sunday,
without thinking about it, and certainly without the least suspicion of the plot, he went out by the south door, and returned
to college by the street called Petty Cury.

Quite as hard to bear as open insults and attempts at
outrage were the coldness and half-expressed contempt of
men of his own standing. Indeed, this must have been to him
the heavier burden of the two. The disorderly undergraduate

challenged and called out his personal courage as well as his patience; the slow trials of social estrangement, surely one of the severest tests of principle to a man of refinement and sensibility, could not be met by action. 'I remember the time that I was quite surprised that a Fellow of my own College ventured to walk with me for a quarter of an hour on the grass-plot before Clare Hall; and for many years after I began my ministry I was "as a man wondered at", by reason of the paucity of those who showed any regard for true religion.'

He records one incident of the inner history of those trying years:

> When I was an object of much contempt and derision in the University, I strolled forth one day, buffeted and afflicted, with my little Testament in my hand. I prayed earnestly to my God that He would comfort me with some cordial from His Word, and that, on opening the book, I might find some text which should sustain me. It was not for direction I was looking, for I am no friend to such superstitions as the *sortes Virgilance*, but only for support. The first text which caught my eye was this: 'They found a man of Cyrene, Simon by name; him they compelled to bear His cross.' You know Simon is the same name as Simeon. What a word of instruction was here – what a blessed hint for my encouragement! To have the cross laid upon me, that I might bear it after Jesus – what a privilege! It was enough. Now I could leap and sing for joy as one whom Jesus was honouring with a participation of His sufferings.

As the preacher suffered reproach, so of course did his disciples. 'Those who worshipped at Trinity Church,' says Sargent, speaking of 1798, 'were supposed to have left common sense, discretion, sobriety, attachment to the established Church, and love for the Liturgy, and almost whatever else is true and of good report, in the vestibule.' 'A Simeonite' was a soubriquet which for many Cambridge generations not merely denoted but satirised a man's religious opinions.

In an old *Gradus ad Cantabrigiam*, of 1803, I find the word
explained: 'A disciple and follower of the reverend and pious Charles Simeon, M.A., Fellow of King's College – in-
ventor of 'Skeletons of Sermons', !! etc, etc, etc.' Thirty
years ago, within my own recollection, the abbreviation 'Sim'
still survived. The first syllable of the word 'pious' has now
succeeded in its place.

Chapter 6

Growing Influence

The storm of opposition and contempt described in the last chapter began to abate within some ten years of the first outburst; though for many a long day afterwards it left its effects in more chronic forms. As late as 1820 James Scholefield, Fellow of Trinity, and a few years later Greek Professor, was Simeon's curate. He lived at Emmanuel House, a picturesque little mansion standing at the back of Emmanuel College, within five minutes' walk from Trinity Church. An old pupil of Scholefield's records thus a recollection of those days: 'He used to take us with him to dear old Simeon's church, and often, as we have walked with him thither, we heard the coarse abuse he met from the idle undergraduates, who rejoiced in nothing more than hooting at Simeon or his curate'.

But in many ways the world of Cambridge soon began to find out the character of the maligned and ridiculed preacher, and was compelled to own that at least he was sincere. He proved himself the active practical philanthropist, when in the close of 1788 England was in great dearth of bread. The poor of the town were provided for, by a subscription to which Simeon largely contributed. But he knew the neighbouring villages intimately, and it occurred to him that they were equally in want, and he offered to undertake the charge of raising and administering relief for them. He took much of the expense and most of the trouble on himself, stirred up the goodwill of others, and every Monday rode out into the country to see that the bakers sold the bread at half-price to the poor people.

'This benevolent and self-denying conduct,' says his old friend, Mrs. Elliott, 'and the personal labour and expense he incurred, made a great impression on the University, and was one of the first things to open their eyes to the real character of the man who had been so much ridiculed and opposed.' They could not but acknowledge, in spite of his eccentricities, that some great and noble principle must be at work within him to occasion such conduct. 'He means well at least,' they said, 'this is not like madness.'

A little earlier, in 1786, he had preached for the first time before the University, in Great St. Mary's Church. It may seem strange that he should have been called there so soon, young as he was and so far from popular. But the system of choice of preachers at that time was very different from what it is now, when more often than not the pulpit is filled by some man of high reputation not resident at Cambridge, and perhaps not a Cambridge man, named by a committee of selection and then invited. In former days two University sermons were preached each Sunday. The afternoons were usually allotted by a special arrangement to well-known senior men, a month to each; Simeon was repeatedly chosen for this work in later life. But the morning sermons were otherwise provided for; the Colleges, in a certain rotation, named successively a man for a Sunday, and it was not unusual for the man named to procure a substitute for the occasion, who might be much his junior. This first sermon of Simeon's, if I am right, was a morning sermon.

Any of my readers who have attended our University Church will in some measure realise that scene; but we shall do so the better if we can picture what the church was like before the great interior alterations were made in 1864. It was a magnificent auditorium, though most anomalously arranged from the strict ecclesiastical point of view. The organ, as now, filled the western arch under the tower, and then, as now, the two aisles of the nave were occupied by spacious galleries, which are thronged with tier upon tier of undergraduate hearers when a popular preacher is in the pulpit. A similar deep gallery then projected from the front of the organ-loft, and opposite to it, filling the chancel arch and almost totally concealing the chancel, towered a gallery still deeper, the place where sat the Vice-Chancellor, Masters of Colleges, Doctors, and Professors. It was known always as the Golgotha, the Place of Heads, a word from which immemorial use had banished irreverence. Under the galleries sat the congregation from the town; and the central space left in the nave was filled with plain benches, set east and west, where sat the Masters of Arts. The pulpit, a tall wooden turret, dark and stately, stood at the western end of this space, facing eastward; it was mounted by an inner and unseen staircase, and a sort of mystery attended the preacher's emergence into daylight at the top, a position whence he perfectly commanded the whole assembly. The service was of the simplest. As the bell of St. Mary's ceased to ring, and the organ pealed its voluntary, the Vice-Chancellor and his brother dignitaries appeared in the Golgotha and took their places, while an Esquire Bedell with his silver mace led the preacher to the pulpit; a metrical psalm, or hymn, was sung; the Bidding Prayer and the Lord's Prayer were read by the preacher, the sermon was delivered, the grace pronounced, and all was over. Such precisely is still the ritual of that plain but solemn ordinance, save only that the procession which used to mount from an invisible vestry, and so issue

into the Golgotha, now crosses the street from the Senate
House and passes up the aisle to the stalls which line the
now open chancel. All is at present much more as it should
be, as regards the proprieties of church arrangement. But there
was a greater human grandeur about the old scene, which
cannot be recalled without some lingering regrets.

Seldom was Great St. Mary's fuller than when Simeon
preached there, as he did repeatedly, in 1786, 1796, 1810,
1811, 1815, 1823, 1831. And never was the attraction of
curiosity stronger than when he ascended that pulpit for the
first time. It was Advent Sunday, December 3. Thus does
Venn describe the occasion to his son:

> On Sunday se'nnight [week] our friend Simeon appeared in St. Mary's
> pulpit. His friends were delighted, his bitterest foes struck dumb,
> and all mistaken in the man. On the Saturday before, Dr. Glynn called
> on him, and desired the favour of his company, and to bring his ser-
> mon with him; telling him he had a critical and a prejudiced audi-
> ence to speak to, and he was his friend, believing him to be a good
> man. Mr. Simeon thankfully accepted the invitation. The Doctor
> heard the sermon, corrected and improved it, and concluded, 'Now,
> Sir, as I am called out, and cannot be at St. Mary's, I am glad I can say
> I have read the sermon, and shall be your advocate wherever I go.'
>   There was a very large congregation, and great attention, though
> it is said there were some who came to *scrape*.[1] Pray much that his
> good may not be evil spoken of.

A fuller account of that memorable sermon is given by Mr.
Carus, as he heard it from his uncle, the Rev. W. Carus Wilston,
who was present:

> The greatest excitement prevailed on this occasion. St. Mary's was
> crowded with gownsmen; and at first there seemed a disposition to
> disturb and annoy the preacher in a manner at that period unhappily

---

1. A once customary interruption at St. Mary's, when the sermon did not please
by matter, style, or length.

not unusual. But scarcely had he proceeded more than a few sentences, when the lucid arrangement of his exordium [opening portion of his sermon], and his serious and commanding manner, impressed the whole assembly with feelings of deep solemnity, and he was heard to the end with the most respectful and riveted attention. The vast congregation departed in a mood very different from that in which it had assembled; and it was evident, from the remarks which were overheard at going out, and the subdued tone in which they were made, that many were seriously affected as well as surprised at what they had heard. Of two young men who had come among the scoffers, one was heard to say to the other, 'Well, Simeon is no fool however!' 'Fool!' replied his companion, 'did you ever hear such a sermon before?'[2]

Simeon had been preparing in many ways for this occasion. 'Before honour is humility', and he had been (in John Thornton's words) 'growing downwards year by year under the stern discipline of difficulty met in the right way, the way of close and adoring communion with God'. His faithful elder friend at Yelling remarks on this again and again in 1785: 'Our dear friend Simeon came over to see me; very much improved and grown in grace; his very presence a blessing.' 'My fears concerning him greatly abate. He appears indeed to be much more humbled, from a deeper knowledge of himself. He is a most affectionate friend and living Christian.' 'Come by Cambridge, and pray spend some time with Mr. Simeon. He follows the Lord fully, as Caleb did. It does me good to be with him.' 'None can bear and receive profit from reproof like him.'

About the same time Simeon himself writes to John Thornton, who had written again, and evidently had given him some of a friend's faithful wounds:

---

2. Yet on that very occasion, when after the benediction Simeon remained some time on his knees, one man was heard to say to another, 'Just look at the hypocrite! what a time he goes on praying.'

A thousand thanks to you, dear Sir, for many valuable observations
in your last letter, especially that which I hope to remember – that
ministers, when truly useful, and more perfectly instructed in the
ways of God, are 'off their speed, and not so full of their success'.
Alas, alas, how apt are young ministers (I speak feelingly) to be
talking of that great letter *I*. It would be easier to erase that letter
from all the books in the kingdom than to hide it for one hour from
the eyes of a vain person. Another observation, in a former letter of
yours, has not escaped my remembrance – the three lessons which
a minister has to learn: 1. Humility. – 2. Humility. – 3. Humility.
How long are we learning the true nature of Christianity! A quiet,
sober, diligent application of one's mind to one's particular calling
in life, and a watchfulness over the evils of the heart, seem very
poor attainments to a young Christian; we must be everywhere and
everything, or else we are nothing in his esteem....

> Your most obliged, most honoured,
> and most affectionate Servant.

In his pocket-book, in 1787, he has written twice over, on
separate pages, in large letters: 'Talk not about myself. Speak
evil of no man.'

Devotional life

Behind all that was busy and public in his life he had striven
from the first to 'labour in secret prayer'. An old and intimate friend, the Rev. R. Housman, who had known him from
1783 onwards, and who looked on Simeon as his own first
guide to Christ, has lifted the veil for a moment from those
labours. Housman, though a Johnian, was for some reason
invited by Simeon to share for a while his rooms in King's;
and nearly sixty years later, when Simeon had gone to his
rest, he gave his recollections of that time to Mr. Carus. 'Never
did I see such consistency, and reality of devotion, such
warmth of piety, such zeal and love. I owe that great and holy

man a debt which cannot be cancelled.' While Housman was in King's, Simeon 'invariably arose every morning, though it was the winter season, at four o'clock; and, after lighting his fire, he devoted the first four hours of the day to private prayer and the devotional study of the Scriptures. He would then ring his bell, and calling in his friend with his servant, engage with them in what he termed his family prayer. Here was the secret of his great grace and spiritual strength. Deriving instruction from such a source, and seeking it with such diligence, he was comforted in all his trials and prepared for every duty.'

This early rising did not come easily to him; it was a habit resolutely fought for and acquired. Finding himself too fond of his bed, he had resolved to pay a fine for every offence, giving half-a-crown to his servant. One morning, as he lay warm and comfortable, he caught himself reasoning that the good woman was poor and that the half-crown would be very useful to her. But that practical fallacy was not to be tolerated; if he rose late again, he would walk down to the Cam and throw a guinea into the water. And so he did, though not without a great struggle, for guineas were not abundant in his purse, and also he had learnt to look on them as 'his Lord's money'. But for his Lord's sake the coin was cast in, and there it lies yet, no doubt, in the river's keeping. Simeon never transgressed in that way again.

Guiding future ministers

Thus he prayed, and thus he preached. Very early also he had begun to teach in a more private way, inviting to his rooms the intending clergymen among his undergraduate friends, and giving them systematic instruction. By 1792 these meetings were in full working order. They are thus described by one who was afterwards his dear friend and faithful curate, and whom he gave up at length to India, Thomas Thomason, of Magdalene:

> Mr. Simeon watches over us as a shepherd over his sheep. He takes delight in instructing us, and has us continually at his rooms. He has invited me to his Sunday evening lectures. This I consider one of the greatest advantages I ever received. The subject of his lectures is Natural and Revealed Religion. These subjects he studies with much pains, reads the fruit of his labours to us, and explains it; we write after him. After labouring and labouring for his young men, that his lectures may be as profitable as possible, he then kneels down and thanks God that He makes them in any degree useful to His 'dear, dear young servants'.

Sermon preparation

Perhaps the most serviceable of all this work in his rooms was the sermon class. He began this before 1794, and it was suggested by his own experience. In those days of difficulty at Trinity Church, when the Sunday afternoon was occupied by the Lecturer, and a Sunday evening sermon was made impossible by the church wardens, and when a week-day evening service was still too bold a challenge to opposition, he used to ride out to help his few neighbouring friends. Venn at Yelling, Berridge at Everton, Hicks at Wrestlingworth, with some others, welcomed him; and he took them in turn, Monday, Tuesday and Wednesday of each week. In these village churches he preached without book, and usually on the text he had handled in Cambridge on the Sunday morning. These repeated expositions led him to try to make each more clear and more interesting than the last; and as with Simeon every purpose issued in conscientious work, he studied hard, quite without help, to arrive at definite principles in the matter. With all his energy he set himself to observe and discover;

and his masterly common sense arrived at maxims and results most true and effective, and which at that time were
very nearly original. He saw that the minister of the Word
must not becloud his text, or wander at will from it, but *let it
speak*. And he saw that the sermon must have a certain unity
of theme and message, and that it must be intelligible, and
that it must be interesting. That great nonconformist preacher,
Mr. Spurgeon, certainly a master of his art, has said that the
pastor who would keep his church full must first 'preach the
gospel', and then preach it with three adverbs in his mind –
earnestly, interestingly, fully. In substance this was Simeon's prescription also, and most certainly his practice.

In the course of these studies how to preach not brilliantly
but usefully, he met with a book which greatly developed
his efforts, and set him definitely to work as a teacher of
preachers. It was Jean Claude's *Essay on the Composition
of a Sermon*.

Claude (1619-1687) was one of the ablest of the great
Huguenot divines of the seventeenth century and for many
years chief minister at Charenton, the Huguenot Canterbury,
where he proved himself Bossuet's worthy controversial rival. At the Revocation of the Edict (1685) the great *temple* at
Charenton was at once pulled down, and the pastor, exiled
from France, took refuge with William of Orange, and laboured at the Hague for the rest of his life. Claude had stated
and explained, with French neatness and precision, his rules
for a successful preparation for the pulpit, and his book had
been translated by the Cambridge Baptist minister, Robert
Robinson, mentioned above. Simeon read the translated Essay, and found with surprise that 'all the chief rules which
Claude prescribes had not only been laid down by himself,
but practised for some years'.

Seeing his own methods, the methods of nature as he held them to be, thus reduced to a convenient system, he resolved to begin to teach them. He abridged the Essay in manuscript, with occasional alterations and additions, and then set to work with a few pupils for the pulpit, taking the Essay as his textbook. His purpose was to make his younger friends intelligent and intelligible preachers, who knew both what they meant to say, and how to say it so as to arrest and reward attention; reminding them at every turn that the pastoral sermon is not to be either a treatise out of place, or an oration developed from the mere starting-point of a text, but a setting forth of God's Word by a commissioned messenger in an assembly of living men. He strove accordingly to train his disciples in the right sort of preparation and also in the most effective delivery; to insist upon care in exposition, clearness of arrangement, and directness of appeal. As to the actual utterance, he advised them to prepare their material fully and carefully, but to leave the wording to the moment of delivery.

By any and every means they were to train themselves to be preachers whose sermons should be always full of matter, formed so as to aid attention and memory, and delivered with a manner perfectly natural.

It is not easy at the present day to realise the independence and almost originality of such a programme, deliberately laid down by an English teacher. The traditions of English preaching had long been curiously artificial. The sermon almost always was either read from the manuscript, or *mandated*, committed to memory and then recited.[1] There was a pulpit manner, a pulpit voice, often quite different from the man's voice in common life. It had come to be thought that a natural and manifest expression of earnestness was in place only in the 'unlicensed meeting, or in the fields'. The church would be almost slighted if there the preacher spoke precisely as he felt and in words direct from the heart.

Simeon's practice and his teaching contradicted all these traditions. And his diligent inculcation of the right method, or at least of the right aim, working outward from a great centre of training for the English pastorate, had a powerful influence in the right direction.

Some of his precepts for the preacher must be quoted. He insisted much on the primary requisite, audibility, and on the surest means to it, articulation. 'Bite your words,' he used to say; warning his scholars of the mistake of slurring consonants and final syllables.

'Avoid a continuous solemnity; it should be as music, and not like a funeral procession.'

'Too great familiarity does not become the pulpit, but a monotonous, isochronous solemnity is even worse.'

'Seek to speak always in your natural voice. You are generally told to speak up; I say rather speak down. It is by the strength not by the elevation of your voice that you are to be heard.'

'Speak exactly as you would if you were conversing with an aged and pious superior. This will keep you from undue formality and from improper familiarity.'

'But the whole state of your own soul before God must be the first point to be considered; for if you yourself are not in a truly spiritual frame of mind, and actually living upon the truths which you preach or read to others, you will officiate to very little purpose'.

In the intense desire to reach the soul and will, he was justly impatient of mere decorations of style. 'Poetry is beautiful in itself,' he says to a friend who had been consulting

him, 'but if you will come from the mount of God, you will
find prose better suited for telling men about their golden
calf.'

All needless circumlocution, and indeed all the devices
of a conventional rhetoric, he despised and discouraged. At
one of his Friday sermon parties, where the men who came
read each his sketch or outline aloud, one unfortunate person
produced the sentence, 'Amidst the tumult of Israel the son of
Amram stood unmoved.'

'The son of Amram, who was he?'

'I meant Moses.'

'Then why not say Moses? What ordinary congregation
carries in their memories genealogies ready for use?'

Simeon's labour in connection with Claude's Essay was
afterwards greatly developed. His Works, as they were published in 1832, fill twenty-one large octavo volumes, and the
title-page reads, *Horce Homileticae: or Discourses (principally in the form of Skeletons) now first digested into one
continued Series, and forming a Commentary upon every
book of the Old and New Testament; to which is annexed an
improved Edition of a Translation of Claude's Essay on the
Composition of a Sermon*. It was the literary achievement of
his life. These volumes contain many discourses fully written, among them the University Sermons; but the majority of
the more than two thousand compositions are precis of parochial sermons, well-ordered outlines of exposition, arranged
according to the books of the Holy Scriptures. The reader, as
the author warns him, will look there in vain for minute criti-
cism or for remote speculation; but he will seldom fail to
gather excellent suggestions how to explain and arrange, and
how to carry messages home from the Word of God to the life
of man. The term 'Skeleton' was certainly unfortunate; as we

saw, Simeon's despisers made merry over it. But the summaries so named were no pieces of lifeless mechanism, as their author planned them, and as he taught others how to use them. They were the bone-systems of sermons which he himself made to live, and speak, and work; and he did his utmost to teach 'his young men' how to do the same.

I reserve for another chapter some further account of Simeon as a preacher, and also as a theologian. And the 'conversation-parties' for which his rooms were famous belong to a later time than the beginnings of his instruction-classes for his pulpit.

Chapter 7

Preacher, Theologian, Churchman

His style of delivery, which to the last was remarkably lively and impressive, in his earlier days was earnest and impassioned in no ordinary degree. The intense fervour of his feelings he cared not to conceal or restrain; his whole soul was in his subject, and he spoke and acted exactly as he felt. Occasionally indeed his gestures and looks were almost grotesque from the earnestness and fearlessness of his attempts to illustrate or enforce his thoughts in detail; but his action was altogether unstudied, sometimes remarkably striking and commanding, and always sincere and serious.

So Carus describes Simeon as a preacher. Another of his old friends, Canon Abner Brown, gives us a similar recollection:

A single remark of Wilberforce's in reference to a specific occasion accurately describes him as at all times; 'Simeon is in earnest'. One could hardly help noticing a peculiar look of earnest reality at all times stamped upon his countenance. His distinct articulation, unlaboured utterance, and accurate pronunciation (except when an occasional school-quaintness occurred in such words as quality, etc), fixed the hearers' attention upon the message, and not on the speaker. His reverential air, his deep unfeigned sincerity, his impassioned reality, his unflagging energy, satisfied the hearers that he deeply felt, and meant to the fullest extent, what he was saying. The correctness of the diction, the frequent eloquence of the style, the honest sincerity, the thoughtful originality, soon compelled even a stranger to forget the peculiarities of manner or gesture, and to listen with deep, often with breathless, attention as to an ambassador from God delivering a powerful and loving message to each hearer individually. Who ever heard a dry sermon from Simeon's lips, or had to listen to a dull remark in conversation with him?[1]

---

1. Recollections of Simeon's Conversation Parties, p. 7.

His English, as shown in his University sermons, where his style is, so to speak, seen at full length, is accurate and strong, a good specimen of the writing of the eighteenth century, when our prose attained a high general standard. It is never ambitious, never ornamented. To be understood, and to come close to the conscience and heart, is the unmistakable purpose everywhere. But the directness and gravity of this purpose keep the language always above tameness, and often lift it to a noble level. I take a specimen, almost at random, from the sermons of 1823. The theme is 'The Excellency and Glory of the Gospel'; and the text, the almost closing words of the third chapter to the Ephesians:

In my text it is said that a view of this sublime mystery will 'fill us with all the fulness of God'. And what can be meant by this? Can it be supposed that a creature should ever resemble God in His *natural* perfections? No; but in His *moral* perfections we both may and must resemble Him, if ever we would behold the face of God in peace. Nay more; we must not only partake of His moral perfections, but must have them all united and harmonising in us, even as they unite and harmonise in God Himself. For instance, while justice, and mercy, and truth, and love, find in us on all occasions their appropriate operations, we must be careful that the opposite graces of faith and fear, humility and confidence, meekness and fortitude, contrition and joy, have full scope not only for occasional, but for constant and harmonious exercise. In a word, we should resemble God, who is light itself. In light, you know, there is an assemblage of widely different rays; some of which, if taken separately, might be thought to approximate rather to darkness than to light. But if the more brilliant rays were taken alone, though they might produce a glare, they would never make light. It is the union of all in their due proportion and in simultaneous motion that constitutes the light; and then only when all the graces are in simultaneous exercise, each softening and tempering its opposite, then only, I say, do we properly resemble God.

The moral force of his preaching, the thrill it sent through the soul, is often commemorated by his friends. One sermon, preached at Edinburgh in 1798, was long remembered for this electric power. It is thus described by one who heard it:

> I remember well his preaching a most striking sermon on ministerial duties and faithfulness, in which he introduced, with a view to illustration, the keeper of the lighthouse on Inch-keith, the island situated in the middle of the Firth of Forth. He supposed the keeper to have let the light go out, and that in consequence the coast was strewed with wrecks and with dead and mangled bodies; and that the wailings of widows and orphans were everywhere heard. He supposed the delinquent brought out for examination before a full court and an assembled people; and at last the answer to be given by him, that he was 'asleep'. – 'Asleep!' The way in which he made his 'asleep!' burst on the ears of his audience, who were hanging in perfect stillness on his lips, contrasting the cause with the effects, I remember to this day.

What follows is characteristic:

> I remember on another occasion in Edinburgh, after having finished an impressive discourse, his standing up with impassioned gesture and stopping a merry jig which was commencing from the organ. He had been preaching in an Episcopalian Chapel on the eternal covenant. As the lively concluding voluntary began, he started from his knees and exclaimed, 'No music! Let the people retire in silence and think upon the covenant!' Perhaps the interruption was ill-judged; but indeed there are voluntaries, and even hymns, which seem only too certain to drive away the impressions of the sermon. To Simeon, the work of the pulpit was inexpressibly important, and he could not politely conceal his sense of this. On another occasion, in Scotland, when 'God had been much with him as he preached', the minister of the church, just after the sermon, in the vestry, began to ask him about his travels. 'Speak to me of heaven, Sir,' he answered, 'and I can talk with you, but do not speak to me about earth at this moment, for I cannot talk about it.' He was quite shocked,

he said, as he told the story at King's one Friday night: 'I cannot bear that matter-of-form spirit which makes the solemnities of God's house, and of worship, a mere business without a reality.'[1]

It has been said that no sermon is what a sermon should be if it is not also *an action*. Simeon's sermons, if any man's, were actions; at once products and incidents of a life which was beyond description real and full.

Canon Brown says that his manner was 'not less attractive to the poor than it was imperative on the attention of the educated, whether they approved or smiled'. In the early days, Trinity Church was attended by many of the villagers from the neglected country parishes near Cambridge. And Brown tells us of an old man, a parishioner of his own in Northamptonshire. John Munn had heard Simeon preach, when in haytime or at harvest he had gone into 'the Fen-country', and often afterwards he craved to hear him again. Every now and then he would say, 'I want to go and hear Mr. Simmons; that's the man as touches my heart! Can't he just preach! And I hanna heard him for six months.' And off he would go, tramping the fifty miles to Cambridge, living as he could, and as often as possible hearing 'Mr. Simmons'.[2]

The soul-moving power of his prime of life was with him to the last. Many years ago the late Dr. Howson, then Dean of Chester, one of Simeon's latest hearers, gave me a vivid reminiscence of his own. Trinity Church was crowded as usual, aisles as well as pews; the pews were not *locked* now. The text was Colossians 1:18: 'That in all things He might have the pre-eminence.' One passage was written for ever on the listener's heart by the prophetic fire of the utterance, as the old man seemed to rise and dilate under the impression of his

---

1. Brown: Recollections, p. 26. 2. Ibid., p. 8.

Master's glory: – 'That He might have the pre-eminence! And He *will* have it! – And He *must* have it! – And He shall *have* it!'

It is not surprising that not only his own church but Great St. Mary's was always thronged to hear him as the years went on. In November, 1811, 'the sight of the overflowing church was almost electric', so says one of his old friends in a private paper before me. In 1814, 'there was scarcely room to move, above or below'; in 1815, the 'audiences were immense; attention candid and profound'. In 1823, when he preached the series from which I quoted just above, many were unable to get inside the doors.

His doctrine

I have already said something of the doctrine which Simeon preached, and by which he lived. Here I offer a somewhat more detailed view of it. Could we have questioned him on his school, his system, his reply would almost certainly have been that his great hope and effort was to be *Biblical*; loyal altogether to the revelation of Scripture, so as to take from it not only his premises but the deductions from them; correcting every inference by that test. And he would have gone on to say that the Articles of his Church were, as a fact, the exact expression of his own deepest convictions on all the great points of Revelation; that he accepted them and held them with all his heart.

If he had been questioned upon his party connection, he would very likely have answered with a most energetic wish (I quote his own words) that 'names and parties were buried in eternal oblivion'. It is plain to the reader of his life that his conversion and early Christian experiences had literally nothing to do with such things. Even of the Methodist movement he had then heard possibly nothing; certainly nothing of Methodist doctrines; nor again of the very existence of the great Church Evangelicals. Venn of Yelling was a discovery to him. And from Venn he would learn nothing at all of the *spirit* of party. From that baneful spirit, altogether different from a faithful and reverent jealousy for distinctive revealed truth, Simeon was kept extraordinarily free all through his life. It is most certain that his sympathies lay, on the whole, with the group of holy and devoted clergymen and laymen who never claimed for themselves the title Evangelical, but who did so dwell upon the central message of the *Evangelium*, Christ Crucified and Risen, as to win from it an honourable soubriquet. His dearest personal friends from first to last were found among them. Their opponents and satirists were also his. But even among them he took a perfectly independent position, *nullius addictus jurare in verba*. And his necessary and affectionate special relations with them were always governed and influenced by his deep and honest loyalty to Scripture, his cordial allegiance to the doctrine and discipline of the English Church as such, and his love of his Redeemer's image wherever he saw it reflected.

His *Biblicism* comes out everywhere in his life and writings. 'I love the simplicity of the Scriptures; and I wish to receive and inculcate every truth precisely in the way, and to the extent, that it is set forth in the inspired Volume.' Were this the habit of all divines, there would soon be an end of most of the controversies that have agitated and divided the Church of Christ. 'My endeavour is to bring out of Scripture what is there, and not to thrust in what I think might be there. I have a great jealousy on this head; never to speak more or less than I believe to the mind of the Spirit in the passage I am expounding.' 'I would run after nothing, and shun nothing.' 'Perhaps you little thought in what you said against the golden mean, that you would carry me along with you. But I go even far beyond you, for to you I can say in words what these thirty years I have proclaimed in deeds, that the truth is not in the middle, and not in one extreme, but in both extremes.'

Calvinism and Arminianism

This last sentence was written to a friend in 1825. He wonders whether the friend will not tremble for his mental soundness. But he explains himself:

> Here are two extremes; observing days, eating meats, etc. – Paul, how do you move? In the mean way? No. – To one extreme? No. – How then? To both extremes in their turn, as occasion requires.
>
> Here are two other extremes, Calvinism and Arminianism (for you need not to be told how long Calvin and Arminius lived before St. Paul). How do you move in reference to these, Paul? In a golden mean? No. – To one extreme? No. – How then? To both extremes; today I am a strong Calvinist, tomorrow a strong Arminian. – Well, well, Paul, I see thou art beside thyself; go to Aristotle, and learn the golden mean.
>
> But I am unfortunate; I formerly read Aristotle, and liked him much; I have since read Paul, and caught somewhat of his strange notions, oscillating (not vacillating) from pole to pole. Sometimes I am a high Calvinist, at other times a low Arminian, so that if extremes will please you, I am your man; only remember, it is not one extreme that we are to go to, but both extremes.
>
> Now, my beloved brother, if I find you in the zenith on the one side, I shall hope to find you in the nadir on the other; and then we shall be ready (in the estimation of the world, and of *moderate* Christians, who love the golden mean) to go to Bedlam together.

What is commonly, though not very accurately, called the Calvinistic controversy, was in vigorous movement all through Simeon's youth and early manhood. It had troubled the stream of the great Methodist revival, when the Wesleys and Whitefield took opposite sides, while the Church Evangelicals on the whole were Calvinistic, or let us say Augustinian, whether to an extreme degree, as Toplady, or with more balance and reserve, as Venn, Newton, and Scott. My own convictions are more with Whitefield and Venn than with their great antagonists, who were also to the last their friends. But who that has ever reverently looked, I will not say into, but upon, the supreme mysteries involved in such a debate, does not soon arrive at the point of silence? And who that really seeks to throw upon these enigmas the light of Scripture, does not feel that Scripture itself, while assuredly it indicates a system, refuses to elaborate one, or to authorise man to elaborate one by deduction into details? The Augustinian, taught in the school of the soul, feels that his assertion of the sovereignty of grace is important in practice because it assigns to the divine mercy the whole praise of every salvation. When he has written that truth large on his faith and his prayers, there is little else for which he much cares to contend in the matter; that is, little which is properly religious as distinct from metaphysical. Such on the whole seems to have been Simeon's attitude in the controversy of his day. 'I am like a man,' he used to say, 'swimming in the Atlantic, and I have no fear of striking one hand against Europe and the other against America.' Under this conviction he shrunk from any but the most cautious deductions, and sought to find common rather than divergent lines.

An extract from the preface to his *Horœ Homileticae* puts some of his deepest convictions before us with characteristic explicitness:

The author is disposed to think that the Scripture system is of a broader and more comprehensive character than some very dog-matical theologians are inclined to allow; and that, as wheels in a complicated machine may move in opposite directions and yet subserve one common end, so may truths apparently opposite be perfectly reconcilable with each other and equally subserve the pur-poses of God in the accomplishment of man's salvation. The author feels it impossible to avow too distinctly that it is an invariable rule with him to endeavour to give to every portion of the Word of God its full and proper force, without considering what scheme it fa-vours, or whose system it is likely to advance. Of this he is sure, that there is not a decided Calvinist or Arminian in the world who equally approves of the whole of Scripture ... who, if he had been in the company of St. Paul whilst he was writing his Epistles, would not have recommended him to alter one or other of his expressions.

But the author would not wish one of them altered; he finds as much satisfaction in one class of passages as in another; and em-ploys the one, he believes, as freely as the other. Where the in-spired Writers speak in unqualified terms, he thinks himself at lib-erty to do the same; judging that they needed no instruction from him how to propagate the truth. He is content to sit as a learner at the feet of the holy Apostles, and has no ambition to teach them how they ought to have spoken.

In this connection let me quote Simeon's report of an in-terview with John Wesley, given in this same preface to the *Horce Homileticae*:

A young minister, about three or four years after he was ordained, had an opportunity of conversing familiarly with the great and ven-erable leader of the Arminians in this kingdom, and, wishing to im-prove the occasion, he addressed him nearly in the following words: 'Sir, I understand that you are called an Arminian; and I have been sometimes called a Calvinist; and therefore I suppose we are to draw daggers. But before I consent to begin the combat, with your per-mission I will ask you a few questions.'

Permission being very readily and kindly granted, the young min-ister proceeded to ask: 'Pray, Sir, do you feel yourself a depraved creature, so depraved that you would never have thought of turning to God, if God had not first put it into your heart?' 'Yes,' says the veteran, 'I do indeed.'

'And do you utterly despair of recommending yourself to God by anything you can do; and look for salvation solely through the blood and righteousness of Christ?' 'Yes, solely through Christ.'

'But, Sir, supposing you were at first saved by Christ, are you not somehow or other to save yourself afterwards by your own works?' 'No, I must be saved by Christ from first to last.'

'Allowing, then, that you were first turned by the grace of God, are you not in some way or other to keep yourself by your own power?' 'No.'

'What then, are you to be upheld every hour and every moment by God, as much as an infant in its mother's arms?' 'Yes, altogether.'

'And is all your hope in the grace and mercy of God to preserve you unto His heavenly kingdom?' 'Yes, I have no hope but in Him.'

'Then, Sir, with your leave I will put up my dagger again; for this is all my Calvinism; this is my election, my justification by faith, my final perseverance: it is in substance all that I hold, and as I hold it; and therefore, if you please, instead of searching out terms and phrases to be a ground of contention between us, we will cordially unite in those things wherein we agree.'

It appears by that wonderful record, John Wesley's Journal, that this interview took place as early as December 20, 1784:

I went to Hinxworth (in Cambridgeshire), where I had the satisfaction of meeting Mr. Simeon, Fellow of King's College in Cambridge. He has spent some time with Mr. Fletcher, at Madeley; two kindred souls, much resembling each other in fervour of spirit and earnestness of their address. He gave me the pleasing information that there are three parish churches in Cambridge wherein true Scriptural religion is preached, and several young gentlemen who are happy partakers of it.

The three churches were probably St. Edward's, St. Giles, of which Farish was then Vicar, and Trinity.

We are told a little, in some notes by Thomason, of Simeon's visit to the heavenly-minded John Fletcher, at Madeley Vicarage.

> As soon as he entered his house, and told him he was come to see him, Mr. Fletcher took him by the hand, and brought him into the parlour, where they spent a few minutes in prayer that a blessing might rest upon his visit.... Away they went to church. Here Mr. Fletcher took a bell, and went through the whole village ringing it, and telling every person he met that they must come to church, for there was a clergyman from Cambridge come to preach to them.

Baptism

Simeon's views of Baptism somewhat varied in the course of his life. His maturest opinions are conveyed in his sermons 'On the Excellency of the Liturgy', preached in 1811 before the University:

> Great, exceeding great benefit accrues to the soul from Baptism. Where the ordinance is really attended upon in faith, and prayer is offered up to God in faith, we do believe that God bestows a peculiar blessing on the child, though we cannot ascertain that He does so but by the fruits that are afterwards produced.... But even from the ordinance itself we may consider great good as arising to the soul, since, as in the case of circumcision, the person is thereby brought into covenant with God. The Israelites, as a nation in covenant with God, were highly privileged; for 'to them', as the Apostle says, 'belonged the adoption, and the glory, and the covenants'.
>
> ....But we must distinguish between a change of state and a change of nature. Baptism is a change of state: for by it we become entitled to all the blessings of the new covenant; but it is not a change of nature. A change of nature may be communicated at the time that the ordinance is administered; but the ordinance itself does not communicate it.... Simon Magus was baptised; and yet remained in the gall of bitterness.... And so it may be with us; and this is an infallible proof, that the change which the Scriptures call the new birth does not of necessity accompany this sacred ordinance.... If only

we will distinguish the sign from the thing signified, and assign to each its proper place and office, there will be an immediate end of this controversy.

Brown records a remark of Simeon's on the same subject at a conversation-party: 'I believe that Baptism is only the investing us with a right, which we shall not possess unless it is sued out in faith.'

The Holy Spirit

His four sermons at St. Mary's on 'The Offices of the Holy Spirit', preached in 1831, are a noble exposition, grave, candid, and soul-searching in the application; a good answer to the statement sometimes made that 'Simeon and his friends said little of the Paraclete'. They were written when the alleged renewal of the Pentecostal miracles in Edward Irving's church[1] in London had called new attention to the gospel of the Holy Spirit and in many earnest minds had discredited the attempt to present it in its sacred fulness. Simeon utters an uncompromising warning against spiritual illusions. 'To be sure,' writes his Quaker friend, Joseph John Gurney, 'thou dost not use the pseudo-gifted ones of the present day very ceremoniously.' But he does not make the deplorable mistake of meeting the distortion of a sublime truth with silence about the truth itself. 'As God has not given the Spirit by measure to our Lord, so is there no measure fixed for the dispensation

---

1. Mrs Tonna, better known by her literary signature, 'Charlotte Elizabeth,' preserves a recollection of an occasion when Simeon and Irving were together on the platform at a religious meeting, soon after Irving's utterance of a peculiar view of the Human Nature of our Lord. Irving suddenly called on the meeting to engage in prayer,while he led them. 'The expression of Simeon's countenance, who can portray? He rested his elbows firmly on his knees, firmly clasped his hands together, placed his chin against his knuckles, and every line in his face, where the lines were neither few nor faintly marked, bespoke a fixed resolve to say Amen to nothing which he had not well sifted and deliberately approved.'

of it to us. It is our privilege not only to "have the Spirit", but to "be filled with the Spirit". Christ came not only that you might have life, but that you might have it more abundantly. Yes, He would have you to live in the Spirit, and walk in the Spirit, and purify your souls by the Spirit, and abound in hope through the Spirit, and be filled with joy in the Holy Ghost. See to it then that you avail yourselves of these immense advantages; and beg of God to pour out His Spirit more and more abundantly on you through Jesus Christ.'

Holiness

I have sometimes asked myself what would be Simeon's view, were he now with us, of those movements in the Church of Christ which in late years have given a special prominence to the great word Holiness. Most surely he would have looked on them with no mere prejudices; the friend of Fletcher could not do so. He would have gone all lengths with Christian teachers who emphasise the summons to the soul, in Christ's name and by His power, to 'sin no more', and who point to the prayer of the Church, 'Keep us this day without sin'. He would have delighted in every testimony to the truth that boundless resources for moral deliverance and victory are laid up for us in our risen Redeemer, ready to be received and used by the hands of faith. 'There is nothing,' he writes somewhere, 'which I more condemn than a proneness to rest in the mere act of complaining, without getting my complaints removed.' His warning or protest would have been heard only if such appeals were anywhere distorted into substitutes for the truths of the Atonement, or into excuses, on whatever principle, for a religious tone which forgets humility and contrition.

In an interview with a group of earnest Christians who

had taken up with a view of Christian perfection which led them to a reluctance to confess sin, he warned them against any theory which 'leads a man to think of his perfection instead of searching out his imperfections'. He felt, and rightly, if the Scriptures are right, that where humility is absent holiness is at least upon the wing. 'I love simplicity; I love contrition. Even religion itself I do not love if it be not cast in a mould of humility. I love the religion of heaven; to fall on our faces while we adore the Lamb is the kind of religion which my soul affects.' But let it not be thought that he did not therefore, true to his own principle, 'go to the other extreme'. I quote a few sentences from a letter of his old age, 'to a friend under religious depression':

> Could I ascend with you into our Father's presence, and fetch fire from the altar before the throne, or, to change the metaphor, could our souls be tuned by the same divine hand, I should understand and feel every note you strike. But I feel I understand nothing of your case, except as far as words ill-comprehended can convey it. Your case is this: 'I was once in earnest about my soul: I have since declined: I feel but cold and unhumbled, while confessing what ought to humble me in the dust. What must I do?'
>
> The general answer to this would be, 'Be much in reading the Holy Scriptures and in heavenly meditations; be much in prayer to God through Christ; read the promises and rely upon them, and cast yourself entirely on Christ as able and willing to save you to the uttermost.' To that purpose I might speak at large; but yet I should say nothing which you do not already know. I will therefore ... touch only on what may not have presented itself to your notice.
>
> There are two errors which are common to persons in your state: First, the using of means as though by the use of them they could prevail; and secondly, the not using of them because they have so long been used in vain. The error consists in putting the means too much in the place of Christ, and in expecting from exertion what is only gained by affiance. There is a passive state of mind, a lying like clay in the hands of the Potter, and a casting yourself on Christ,

content to sink if He will let you sink, and to be marred, if He choose to mar you. This willingness to be saved by Him altogether from first to last, and in His own time and way, and this determination to trust in Him though He slay you, and to praise Him though He condemn you, is what you particularly want.

There is another thing.... You are too much occupied in looking at yourself and too little in beholding the Lord Jesus Christ. It is by the former you are to be humbled; but it is by the latter that you are to be changed into the divine image. You want a greater measure of holiness to warrant your confidence in the divine promises; when it is only by apprehending those promises that you can attain the holiness you are seeking after (2 Corinthians 7:1). You must learn to glory in your infirmities, that the power of Christ may rest upon you. You are nothing, and it discourages you; but you must be content to be nothing, that Christ may be all in all.

Such sentences might have come from Guyon's pen in a letter to Fenelon, on *La Voie passive en Foi*.

Perhaps the English Church never had a more loving and devoted son and servant than Simeon. From the first to the last of his Cambridge life he was, in Brown's words, 'resolutely and unceasingly anxious that all men should love and venerate the Church of England, instead of watching and spying out her faults, which were, he said, at the worst, no more than "spots upon the sun's disk". He would say, "Seek not to change even what you deem faulty, for hardly any change could be effected in the Prayer-book which would not result in greater evils than those which you wish to remedy. You cannot realise the evil results to England of any material alteration in the Book of Common Prayer; no other human work is so free from faults as it is".'[1] In the use of that Book in public worship he found one of his purest joys. We saw how its prayers became 'marrow and fatness to his soul'

---

1. Recollections, p. 62.

after his conversion; and so they remained: 'Never do I find myself nearer to God than I often am in the reading-desk.' 'The finest sight short of heaven would be a whole congregation using the prayers of the Liturgy in the true spirit of them.'[1]

He deplored the coldness and slackness of Church life in the country generally, and he looked on its real resuscitation as one of the sacred objects of his own labours. And I cannot but think that not a little of the revived consciousness of corporate life and duty in the national Church, often attributed almost wholly to the movement which Simeon lived to see begin at Oxford, is due to his persistent work and witness at the other centre of academic influence.

It is sometimes said that Simeon and his friends exaggerated the subjective side of religion, and only faintly recognised the objective side. But was it so? They never made emotion, or even spiritual experience, their basis, or their test. And never certainly did Simeon fail in loyalty to the objectivity, not only of the written Word of God, but of the historic Ministry and Sacraments.

He held that the Christian minister is quite distinctively God's ambassador; not indeed a mediator, but an appointed means. He said of the Benediction: 'In pronouncing it, I do not do it as a mere finale, but I feel that I am actually dispensing peace from God, and at God's command. I know not the individuals to whom my benediction is a blessing; but I know that I am the appointed instrument by whom God is conveying the blessing to those who are able to receive it.'[2]

A passage from the close of his sermons on 'The Excellency of the Liturgy' is in point here:

1. Recollections, p. 221.
2. Ibid., p. 89.

What might not be hoped for, if all who have undertaken the sacred office of the ministry fulfilled their engagements in the way we have described? What if all prayed the prayers instead of reading them, and laboured out of the pulpit as well as in it? If there were such exertions made in every parish, we should hear no more complaints about the increase of dissenters.... Let me not be misunderstood, as though I meant to suggest anything disrespectful of the dissenters; for I honour all that love the Lord Jesus in sincerity, of whatever Church they be, and I wish them, from my heart, every blessing that their souls can desire. But whilst I see such abundant means of edification in the Church of England, I cannot but regret that any occasion should be given to men to seek for that in other places which is so richly provided for them in their own Church. Only let us be faithful to our engagements, and our churches will be crowded, our sacraments thronged, our hearers edified; good institutions will be set on foot; yea, and our wilderness world will rejoice and blossom as the rose.'

We shall see later what was his brotherly respect for Christians of non-episcopal churches. Like Hall, Hooker, and Jewell, he was able to maintain the most convinced and deliberate preference and allegiance without distorting it into a narrow and futile excommunication.

Chapter 8

India – Religious Societies

Beside me lies a paper, preserved among other documents of Simeon's life, which carries us from Cambridge and England to his work for India. On the outside he has written: 'Address to me from India, relative to a Mission to Calcutta, Sept., 1787. It merely shows how early God enabled me to act for India, to provide for which has now for forty-one years been a principal and an incessant object of my care and labour.... I used jocosely to call India my *Diocese*. Since there has been a Bishop, I modestly call it my *Province*.'

The paper is a letter, or memorial, to the young man of twenty-eight:

REVEREND SIR,
From the enclosed papers you will learn the project of a Mission to the East Indies. We understand such matters lie very near your heart, and that you have a warm zeal to promote their interest. Upon this ground we take the liberty to invite you to become Agent on behalf of the intended Mission at home.... We are much concerned that the Missionaries sent out to this country may be of the right sort. A subsistence equal to £50 per annum in England is all that is held out to them. We therefore hope they will not propose to themselves great earthly emoluments, that their reward may be great in heaven. Should there be a disposition in the higher powers to embrace the scheme, perhaps it would be advisable to have some chosen men in readiness to offer themselves to engage in the work, which might prevent improper applications. Any new matter that may occur to us upon the subject will be transmitted to you by the next ships.

Accept, dear Sir, our best wishes for your success. Our prayer will be continually offered up for a rich blessing upon this and every

92   CHARLES SIMEON

other work in which you may be engaged for the furtherance of the
blessed Gospel of Jesus Christ.

We are, Reverend Sir,

Your most obedient and humble Servants,

D. BROWN, Minister at the Orphan House.

WM. CHAMBERS,

CHAS. GRANT,   Of the Company's

And for GEO. UDNY   Civil Service

Calcutta,
Septr., 1787.

David Brown, of Magdalene, a few years Simeon's junior,
and his friend, had gone out to Bengal as chaplain in 1786. In
1794 he was appointed 'Chaplain to the Presidency', and in
1800 Provost of the College of Fort William. He died in
1812, the year of the death of his beloved Indian colleague
Henry Martyn, leaving a memory bright with consistent goodness and able and unwearied labour for his Lord. The three
other signatories were all distinguished civilians, early members of that long succession of Christian administrators which
has thrown the light of godliness on many passages of the
history of British India. Mr. Grant (of whom more shall be
said later) was father of Charles and Robert Grant, second
and third Wranglers when Martyn was Senior, men afterwards
illustrious in Indian annals as Lord Glenelg and Sir Robert
Grant.

The 'Scheme' was the establishment of two Missionaries
at Benares. The proposed salary for each was raised later to
£150.

This was not the first effort by Englishmen for the conversion of India. Already in 1658 the Directors of the East India
Company recorded their desire 'by all possible means to
propagate the Gospel in those parts'. In 1677 they sent out a
schoolmaster, who was to instruct native children, with oth-

ers, 'in the Protestant religion'. The Charter of 1698 provided that the chaplains of garrisons and factories should 'learn the native language, the better to instruct in the Protestant religion the Gentoos that shall be servants or slaves of the Company or of their agents'. Early in the eighteenth century the first Protestant missionaries, Lutherans, sailed from Denmark; they were supported in England by the Society for Promoting Christian Knowledge. In 1750 the apostolic Swartz landed in Southern India, and when he died in 1798 the East India Directors placed his statue, by Flaxman, in the chief church at Madras; the epitaph set forth his missionary labours, and they ordered its purport to be circulated in the country languages. Clive himself, in 1758, invited to Bengal its first Protestant missionary, Kiernandier. But when the Memorial to Simeon was sent from Calcutta, Lord Cornwallis was Governor-General, and he was lukewarm at best; he 'had no faith in such schemes'. And the two missionaries were not to be found, even by Simeon's efforts.

In the Charter of 1793 Wilberforce asked to insert a clause owning the duty of England to seek the 'religious and moral improvement of the native inhabitants of the British dominions in India'. The Commons passed it, but the Company successfully opposed. Sir John Shore, afterwards Lord Teignmouth, succeeded Lord Cornwallis; an earnest Christian and a warm friend of Missions. But he was compelled to recognise the impossibility, or at least the grave mischief, even from the missionaries' point of view, of using the authority of Government in any degree in their favour. Lord Mornington, afterwards Marquis Wellesley, succeeding Sir John Shore, was equally friendly to the work and even disposed to promote it in his public character. But troubles in the Madras Presidency raised a panic at Calcutta, and the first few years of the nineteenth century, and particularly the two years before 1813, saw the Bengal Government actually hostile to missionaries. The great Baptist scholars and evangelists, Carey, Marshman, and Ward, could live and work only at Serampore, a Danish station near Calcutta. The noble-hearted American, Judson, in 1812, had no sooner landed than he was ordered away; and he crossed the Bay of Bengal to live and die as the evangelist of Burma. But happier days were at hand. The efforts of Wilberforce and his Clapham friends at last succeeded, and the Charter of 1813 provided for a Bishopric at Calcutta, and for the freedom of missionary enterprise in all the territories of the Company.

This brief sketch will serve at least to explain why Simeon in his long care for India sent out chaplains rather than missionaries. The one missionary proper among his followers was William Jowett, B.D., tenth Wrangler in 1810, and Fellow of St. John's. He went to the Levant in September, 1815, and laboured in Syria and Palestine till 1830. But Buchanan, Corrie, Martyn, Thomason, Hough, Dealtry, all were chaplains. The reason was evident. Missionaries in British India at the best would have laboured under severe restrictions. Chaplains had a status in which they could at least learn the native tongues, and translate the Scriptures, without political interference.

From 1786 to 1836 India was near to Simeon's heart; India, then more distant in respect of communication than the remotest depths of 'darkest Africa' now are. In 1813, at the critical time of the renewal of the Charter, he writes to Thomason, then in India: 'On the subject of facilitating the diffusion of Christian light in India there are going to be petitions from all quarters.[1] Vast opposition is made to it; Lord

1. About 1,500 were actually present.

Castlereagh is adverse to it; examinations are making in relation to it at the bar of the House of Commons: Hastings is
very adverse.'

In 1814 he discusses with Thomason the 'use of the Koran
and the Shaster' in Missionary Schools, and agrees with him
that it is 'perfectly right'; and further tells him that 'the Directors had entered a philippic for you'; but it was stopped
by the Board of Control.

In 1820 he is writing to him about new developments of
work: 'I have received your reports, and firstfruits of the
labours of your Tract Society. What a glorious work it is; to
see so much talent called forth and combined, in such a variety of ways, and to such a vast extent.... All your proceedings about the Orphan House, and the kind of tracts to be
written for the natives, and your editing of Euclid, my soul
goes along with you in every atom of it.'

In 1835 he writes a careful and able letter to Wilson, Bishop
of Calcutta, upon that grave problem for Indian missionaries,
caste, and says that he 'would rather undermine the horrid
structure than have it butted down at once'.

The Church Missionary Society

The 'Scheme' of 1787 proved for the present abortive. But it
was the introduction to greater enterprises. Charles Grant
came home in 1790, and pressed the missionary duty upon
Archbishop Moore and the Bishop of London, and through
them upon the King. His appeals were met with a caution
which may now seem scarcely credible; but their effect was
felt when Wilberforce agitated the matter in Parliament in
1793; and, what was most important of all just then, the souls
of the wise and good men who at Cambridge and Clapham
thought and acted with Wilberforce were effectually set on

fire with what may be called the missionary consciousness. They resolved that something extensive and systematic should at last be attempted in the English Church for the evangelisation of the heathen and Mahometan peoples.

Already there existed the great Societies for the Propagation of the Gospel and the Promotion of Christian Knowledge. But their appointed field was the British Colonies, not the pagan world as such. The admirable work of the London Missionary Society had recently been begun. But its constitution was unsectarian, and its Anglican members found that it would be better for all parties that the ecclesiastical difference should be recognised candidly, while personal Christian friendship and all possible co-operation on parallel lines should be maintained. So the thought of a Society within the Church of England with a purely missionary purpose rose in many minds, and the issue of it was 'the Church Missionary Society for Africa and the East', or, as it was called in its first Account, 'A Society for Missions to Africa and the East, instituted by members of the Established Church'.

Simeon's part in the origination of the CMS was important. In the spring of 1795 he was present at a clerical meeting at Rauceby in Lincolnshire where the disposal of a bequest of £4,000, left for religious purposes, was debated, and some suggested its use for missions. In September, at the same place, the question was opened again, and Simeon tabulated with characteristic precision the arguments on both sides, which left the matter still uncertain. In February, 1796, the subject came before 'the Eclectic'. This was a Clerical Society meeting in London, and the rendezvous of such men as John Venn, Richard Cecil, Thomas Scott and Josiah Pratt. At that February meeting Simeon reported the bequest, and a conversation followed, hesitating in its tone and without direct results; the fear of episcopal disapproval, and of a seeming interference with old societies, was so strong. But the discussion helped to keep the question alive, and three years later, March 18, 1799, a more resolute and effectual treatment of it was possible. Simeon had been expressly asked to attend the Eclectic, and Charles Grant was there also as a visitor:

Fourteen members were present. Mr. Venn opened the discussion, by insisting upon the duty of doing something for the conversion of the heathen. Mr. Charles Grant urged the founding of a Missionary Seminary.... The Rev. Charles Simeon, with characteristic distinctness of purpose and promptitude of zeal, proposed three questions: 'What can we do? When shall we do it? How shall we do it?

'(i.) What can we do? We cannot join the (London) Missionary Society; yet I bless God that they have stood forth. We must now stand forth. We require something more than resolutions, something ostensible, something held up to the public. Many draw back, because we not stand forward.

'(ii.) When shall we do it? Directly; not a moment to be lost. We have been dreaming these four years, while all England, all Europe, has been awake.

'(iii.) How shall we do it? It is hopeless to wait for Missionaries. Send out Catechists.'

The result of this meeting was a general consent that a Society should be forthwith formed, by inviting a few of those upon whose concurrence in their own views they could rely; and that a prospectus of their proceedings should be afterwards prepared, and that then their plans should be laid before the heads of the Church. The next meeting of the Eclectic was devoted to the same subject, and the rules of the proposed Society were considered and settled. On the 12th of April a meeting was held at the Castle and Falcon Inn, Aldersgate Street, 'For the purpose of Instituting a Society amongst the Members of the Established Church for sending Missionaries among the Heathen'. The Rev. J. Venn was in the chair, and detailed the objects of the meeting. Sixteen clergymen and nine laymen were all that composed that small assembly; but the blessing of God was

manifestly with them in their 'work of faith and labour of love'.
'The Society for Missions to Africa and the East', then formally
established, grew and advanced like the grain of mustard-seed.[1]

That memorable meeting of the Eclectic was summoned when,
between the Nile and Marengo, England was in the midst of
the universal War,

> When the century in tempest vanish'd,
> And the next in carnage stalk'd behind.

And it was a meeting of men who for the most part were held
of little account in either the world or the Church. Yet they
were equally sober and confident, in the name of God; and
He has justified their act of faith.

The first secretary of the new Society was Thomas Scott,
then Chaplain of the Lock Hospital; once an almost Socinian
curate, eager only to study, then gently led by John Newton to
adore his Redeemer, and at this time already a strong and
patient leader in Christian enterprises. Just before one of the
first small annual meetings of the Society a young clergyman asked Scott, a little carelessly, how they were getting
on with money and men. 'We have collected about £1200,'
was the answer, 'and we have hopes of an offer of service
from two German students.' A smile came into the question-
er's face, and Scott turned solemnly upon him: 'Young man,
you don't believe in this work. But if you live to be as old as
I am, mark the word, you will see our missionaries enter
China and Japan'; regions then 'hermetically sealed', as Japan continued to be for sixty years. The prophecy proved
true; and the story was told me by a friend, who had heard it
from a venerable pastor, once the incredulous young ques-
tioner of Thomas Scott.

---

1. Quoted from a Memorandum drawn up by Archdeacon Pratt of Calcutta.

Simeon preached the second Annual Sermon of the Society, at St. Anne's, Blackfriars, June 8, 1802. The text was from the Philippian Epistle, where the Apostle points to the infinite Humiliation of the Son of God as the supreme example of unselfish toil and sacrifice. I give one brief quotation:

> It may be said, perhaps, Why are we to waste our strength upon the heathen? Is there not scope for the labours of all at home? I answer, It is well for us that the Apostles did not argue thus; for it they had not turned to the Gentiles till there remained no unconverted Jews, the very name of Christ would probably long since have been forgotten amongst men. Besides, the more our love abounds towards the heathen, the more will the zeal of others be provoked for the salvation of our neighbours; and the more confidently may we hope for the blessing of God upon their pious endeavours. Let then all excuses be put away, and let all exert themselves at least in prayer to the great 'Lord of the harvest', and entreat Him day and night 'to send forth labourers into His harvest'.

In 1817 I find record of the departure of seventeen missionaries of the Society, all Germans, setting sail for their fields of labour; Simeon gave the farewell address. In 1818, he rejoices to think of 'ladies at work in India as in England'. In the same year, in November, he sends to Thomason the news of the first Church Missionary meeting in Cambridge: 'You will be surprised to hear that we have just had a public meeting for the Missionary Society. I trembled when it was proposed, and recommended that the most cautious proceedings.... There were present about 900 persons and 120 gowns.... The meeting was very solemn, the Queen's (Queen Charlotte's) death being announced in the papers that morning.'

I subjoin the close of that letter, though the subject is not in its place here:

As for my church, there is nothing new. Those who so greatly distressed me are gone, and my church is sweetly harmonious. As for the gownsmen, never was anything like what they are at this day. I am forced to let them go up into the galleries, which I never suffered before; and notwithstanding that, multitudes of them are forced to stand in the aisles for want of a place to sit down. What thanks can I render to the Lord for a sight of these things? I am ready to sing my ancestor's song, Luke ii.

Simeon's work for India, though it was thus so closely connected with the origin of a great Missionary Society, was, however, chiefly done through the able and pious Cambridge men whom he recommended as chaplains to the East India Company. Without some record of them no view of his religious leadership would be complete; Martyn, Thomason, and their Indian brethren from Cambridge were living extensions of Simeon's faith and labour. But I keep this record for another chapter, and with it some account of other friends of Simeon's. Here, *a propos* of the Church Missionary Society, let me say a little of other similar works into which Simeon threw much zeal and effort: the British and Foreign Bible Society, and the Society for Promoting Christianity among the Jews.

Mission to the Jews

The Conversion of the Jews was perhaps the warmest interest of his life, in the way of extended religious enterprise. In May, 1813, he tells Thomason that the Bishop of London is about to consecrate 'the new chapel which is building for the Jews Society at Bethnal Green; and that the Archbishop of Canterbury has expressed regret at not having given them his countenance before. For this society I am much interested, being one of the trustees for the chapel. The laying of the first stone about three weeks ago was a most interesting scene. The Duke of Kent laid it, and Lord Erskine, Lord Dundas, Mr. Wilberforce, etc., assisted with a silver trowel. Other buildings will afterwards be added, for the lodging and employing the children that have been baptised, and the adults that went employment. A rich Jew on the Continent has been converted, and he is preaching among his brethren. He is a merchant, who has five different concerns in five different cities... This day brings me tidings of another rich Jew embracing the Christian faith. O that the whole nation might remember themselves, and turn to the Lord!'

Next year he is energetically at work, along with Mr. Lewis Way, over an important rearrangement of the management of 'the Jews Society, which had fallen into some disorder'. With a plan drawn up by Mr. Babington, he writes again to Thomason, 'I proceeded to town; but as that was only one plan, I drew up four others. One was discussed for five hours. To get every possible advice we went to Mr. Wilberforce, at Barham Court in Kent, and under his roof I formed a fifth. This was unanimously adopted, and the Society is placed on a firmer basis than ever. I expect now that some of our higher churchmen will come in, and all the serious clergy throughout the land.'

In 1818 he describes one of the only two visits he ever paid to the Continent. It was to Holland, where he went, travelling with Mr. Marsh (the late Rev. W. Marsh, D.D.), 'most loveable of men', to see with his own eyes the missions to the Jews in the Low Countries, and particularly to support and stimulate the work at Amsterdam. The later visit was to Paris in 1822, and the same cause was in his heart. On that occasion, by the way, he met the Duchesse de Broglie, Mme. de Stael's gifted and eminently Christian daughter, the

friend of Thomas Erskine of Linlathen. 'I opened to her,' he
writes, 'my views of the Scripture system, ... and showed her
that brokenness of heart is the key to the whole.' There was
'a Jews' Meeting at Mr. Way's', and among others present
there Simeon met 'M. Merle d'Aubigne, Protestant minister
at Versailles', afterwards the historian of the Reformation.

Literally to the last the thought of the recovery of Israel to
the divine Messiah was on Simeon's heart. As he lay on his
death-bed, in 1836, the annual Cambridge meeting of the Society drew near, and he resolved to deliver his 'dying testimony to the immense importance of the cause', in a paper to
be read at a gathering of undergraduates. 'I wish to show
you,' so the brief document ran, 'what grounds we have for
humiliation, in that we have been so unlike to God in our
regards towards His fallen people. See Jeremiah 12:7; and
again Romans 11:28. And to bring you into a conformity to
God in relation towards them, so far as it respects your efforts for their welfare, and your joy in their prosperity, see
Ezekiel 36:22-24. And again Jeremiah 32:41. And lastly see
Zephaniah 3:17.' All the Scriptures cited are dictated at full
length in the paper.

British and Foreign Bible Society

His part in the mighty enterprise of the British and Foreign
Bible Society (founded in 1804) was chiefly that of the wise
and energetic adviser on the first introduction of the Society
into Cambridge, and the steady friend of its cause there afterwards. There were serious difficulties in the way when, in
1811, the first 'Bible Meeting' was proposed. Some influential seniors in the University were strongly adverse, and many
of the undergraduates who usually followed Simeon were
ready for an impatient assertion of their feelings and resolves.

The narrative as he writes it to Thomason is remarkable:

> I said in my last page that I would proceed to tell you about my sermons; but I have a matter of infinitely greater importance to communicate, and with that I will now proceed in a way of narrative. At the time I wrote my last sheet, some young men in the University were endeavouring to set forward a Bible Society in Cambridge, and I had determined to call the attention of the seniors to it in my last sermon. But the young men, full of ardour, had gone to the Vice-Chancellor (Dr. Browne of Christ's) and to the Bishop of Bristol (Dr. Mansel), and to Dr. Milner, and some others, to try to interest *them*. A great alarm was excited through the University, and every person without exception threw cold water upon it, from this principle, that if they were suffered to proceed in this way about the Bible, they would soon do the same about politics. This so discouraged me that I almost determined to blot out what I had written. But as I had written it for God, I at last resolved to deliver it for God, in hopes that God might yet do something by it. My view was to the seniors only; I never dreamed of its being serviceable in any other way. But how unsearchable are the ways of God! The young men bowed with perfect willingness to me, and suffered me to draw a line around them beyond which they were not to move. They drew back, and committed everything to their seniors, having indeed professed a willingness to do so from the beginning, but manifestly determined to have more hand in it than would perfectly consist with academic discipline. When their readiness to recede was known, instantly Dr. Jowett, Mr. Farish, Mr. John Brown of Trinity, and myself, stood forward. Mr. F. went to get the sanction of the Vice-Chancellor, who, though he could not say he approved of the measure, gave his consent that a Meeting should be called of the University, Town, and County, for the purpose of establishing a Society.

The troubles were not at an end, however. Herbert Marsh, then Margaret Professor, afterwards Bishop of Peterborough, no admirer of Simeon's, was decidedly hostile to the Bible Society on the ground of its independence of the Church; and he, 'with incredible industry', circulated a strong printed state-

ment of his objections in and around Cambridge. No Head of
a College would promise to attend the meeting; not even
Milner of Queens, 'unless the Bishop of Bristol would'; and
the Bishop of Bristol hesitated, because 'it was in the Bishop
of Ely's diocese'. The meeting had been announced, and it
was close upon the day; what was to be done? Simeon owns
that he 'would at that time have given a large sum that we had
not stirred at all; and so would my colleagues; and if it had
been possible to have recalled the letters and notices, we
should have done it'. But it was not possible. Happily, in this
strait, so difficult to be understood now, but so grave as things
were then, unlooked-for support was promised. Bishop
Mansel and Dean Milner reconsidered their scruples and came
forward, and a great and successful meeting was held. I find
it noticed in Cooper's *Annals of Cambridge*, as the last public event of 1811:

> The Cambridge Auxiliary Bible Society was established at a crowded
> and unanimous public meeting, held at the Town Hall, on the 12th of
> December. The Earl of Hardwicke was in the chair. Amongst the
> speakers were Lord Francis Godolphin Osborne, M.P. for the County,
> Rev. Dr. E.D. Clarke, Professor of Mineralogy, Rev. William Farish,
> M.A., Professor of Chemistry, William Hollick, Esq., Rev. Charles
> Simeon, M.A., Fellow of King's College, Dr. Isaac Milner, Dean of
> Carlisle and President of Queens' College, and Rev. William Dealtry,
> Fellow of Trinity College. The proceedings appear to have excited
> the most intense interest.

Mr. Carus preserves a striking picture, given him by an
eye-witness, an undergraduate of that time, of Simeon's action in private, when the juniors, eager for the meeting, were
in the act of taking an unwise line of resistance to University
authority. They formed a Committee; it was happily proposed
that its first act should be to send a deputation to Simeon:

He was then in those rooms which he had on the ground floor at the foot of the staircase nearest to Queens. The interior of his study, his own form and manner, and the appearance of the whole group, are before me at this time. The gentleness and delicacy and calm strength of his statements and reasoning quite surprised me. I was not prepared to expect that he could exercise so irresistible an influence (as it seemed to me) over the faculties and wills of others, and all without seeming to attempt any influence at all, but only to show how his own mind had been brought to the conclusion at which he arrived. It was not a time for the expression of his affections, as you know he was wont to express them, but the influence of his unexpressed affection was all powerful, though it is likely that the parties before him perceived not the subtle influence of that secret spell which was gradually overmastering their previously settled resolution. For it must be remembered that no one of the three had come with any wavering of mind as to the right course, but only in deference to my urgent representations that it was not just for them to decide without personal conference with him from whom I had my information and my views. I sat in astonishment; I could have wept for joy and wonder. The effect was decisive upon two of my colleagues. From that hour no further question was entertained as to the juniors acting alone; no more meetings were held even of our Committee; the whole was left with unhesitating confidence to the seniors.

Chapter 9

Henry Martyn and Other Friends

I come to some account of Simeon's Indian chaplains. Looking back from the year 1829, he writes, in a private paper, 'Almost all the good men who have gone to India as chaplains these forty years have been recommended by me.' This was not a vainglorious boast; it was a plain fact, recorded with surprise and thankfulness. Unlikely as it seems, Simeon was able, for nearer fifty than forty years, to exercise a strong influence on the East India Company's choice of chaplains; and that long opportunity he used with an insight and a faith which alone might entitle him to the name of a great man as well as a good one.

If I gather up the scattered facts rightly, his friend David Brown, mentioned above, was one of the first links in this chain of circumstances. In 1786, Brown had sailed for India as a Company's chaplain; not, so far as I am aware, because Simeon had advised his going. But he went as a devoted pastor, who could not possibly view with indifference the shepherdless millions of Bengal, and he went as Simeon's friend. At Calcutta he found a Christian coadjutor in Charles Grant; and so Simeon's name was soon familiar in Grant's ears. Grant, returning to England, as we have seen, took his place among the Directors of the Company at home[1], and finding some kindred souls among his colleagues, made them also acquainted with the Cambridge clergyman's character, and

---

1. Macaulay says, in 1844, 'Grant ruled India from Leadenhall Street.' – Life of Lord Macaulay, I. 67, note.

prepared them to look to him for able and earnest chaplains among his disciples at the University.

One of Simeon's first recommendations carried a name now for ever memorable in Christian history, the name of Henry Martyn. For Martyn's own sake, and for that of his inseparable connection with Simeon, we must linger a little over his life and character.

Henry Martyn was born at Truro on February 18, 1781, and baptised in the Church of St. Mary, now the Cathedral, where he is registered as the 'son of John and Elizabeth Martyn'. John Martyn, early in life, had been a working superintendent in the mines at Gwenap, but he had risen by methodical industry and self-education to be chief clerk in a merchant's office in Truro, with an income 'more than competent'. His children were many, but all died quite early save four, two sons and two daughters. Henry was the third child of these four. The younger of the two sisters is often mentioned in his 'Memoir' as exercising a strong religious influence on him during his college life; she was 'in Christ' before him, and prayed unweariedly for him, at a time when he was indifferent to the highest things. At school he had a good classical training, and he was known there as clever but not diligent, usually very cheerful, high-spirited, sometimes passionately angry. He made one good friend at school, an older and stronger boy, known to us only as K; for John Sargent, the writer of Martyn's delightful 'Memoir', never gives us more than his initial. Henry Martyn competed for a scholarship at the Oxford Corpus Christi, but failed; and his father entered him at St. John's College, Cambridge, as a pensioner, or unassisted student. K had gone up there before him, and was his best friend at college as at school.

I have heard, from a distinguished veteran clergyman, to

whom it was told long ago by a friend, once Martyn's teacher
at Cambridge, a story which would defy belief if it had not
such a direct tradition. It was that when the Cornish lad, arriving at St. John's in October, 1797, was examined in his
school acquirements, his classics passed muster well enough,
but so total was his ignorance of mathematics that the first
proposition of the first Book of Euclid quite baffled him.
Such at last was his mental despair that he was on the point
of leaving Cambridge. It was actually as he went to take a
place in the coach which started from the Hoop, the 'famous
inn' where Wordsworth had 'alighted just ten years before',
that the geometrical mystery opened itself to him! However,
he quickly made up these very long arrears.

In January, 1801, in a 'year of high calibre', he was Senior Wrangler and first Smith's (mathematical) Prizeman.
Woodall of Pembroke came next to him in both these distinc-
tions. Robert and Charles Grant, sons (as we have seen) of
Charles Grant, the East India Director, were third and fourth
Wranglers and second and first Chancellor's Classical Med-
allists respectively. Martyn, with whom language and literature were always the dearest study, soon afterwards won the
first University prize for a Latin Essay; Charles Grant received the second. In 1802 he was chosen Fellow of St. John's,
and did good work there as lecturer and examiner.

Meanwhile to him, as to Simeon, Cambridge had been the
place of the great spiritual change. It came 'not with observation'. He was at first so careless of religion that he never
thought of praying in private. So strong were his occasional
bursts of passion that once in the dining hall he hurled a knife
at a neighbour who had provoked him; it missed the man, and
stood trembling in the panel of the wall. But in his third year
at college the death of his father, a desolating grief, led him

to think and pray; his sister's letters and her prayers were not in vain; he found his way to Trinity Church; and already before his degree he had quietly taken his place among those who owned Christ for Master. In October, 1803, he was ordained at Ely, on the title of his Fellowship; like Simeon, he was not yet of canonical age at his ordination. To Simeon he had been drawn, and Simeon to him, with a great depth and warmth of affection; and he served as curate at Trinity Church for nearly two years, taking charge also of the small parish of Lolworth, north-west of Cambridge.

Simeon's heart was full of India at this time, and Martyn had fallen in also with the *Memoir of David Brainerd*, the saintly evangelist, sixty years before, of the Redmen of New England. In the end he felt and owned the call to a missionary life, and Simeon sent his name to the East India Directors. The two friends each showed, in a different way, a noble faith and loyalty towards their Lord – Martyn, in choosing what was then a far distant exile as the next step after his brilliant successes, Simeon, in speeding the departure of a man so gifted for influence in Cambridge, and to himself so dear.

In July, 1805, Martyn sailed from England. Cambridge he had left in April; one of his last farewells was to the beautiful Wilderness, or Fellows Garden, of St. John's, 'where he had often enjoyed communion with God', and which his memory still hallows. He sailed with the fleet which carried to the Cape the soldiers who in January, 1906, wrested the Colony from Holland for England; after the decisive fight, visiting the field, he was nearly killed while ministering to a dying man. Not till the next May did he land at Calcutta. There he saw Carey, and soon afterwards David Brown welcomed him to his house and his heart. He applied himself at once to Hindustani with immense diligence and all his native turn for language; and within a year he was on his way to a mastery which he afterwards proved in his Hindustani New Testament. From Calcutta he was transferred to Dinapore, up the Ganges, and there laboured diligently for the Europeans in the station and its large district, meanwhile studying Sanskrit, Persian and Arabic with all his might. In April, 1809, he was moved to Cawnpore. There Captain Sherwood received him to a warm Christian friendship; and Mrs. Sherwood, the authoress of many books which used to delight the young, has recorded some of her memories of Henry Martyn:

> I perfectly remember the figure of that simple-hearted and holy young man when he entered our bungalow. His features were not regular, but the expression was so luminous, so intellectual, so affectionate, so beaming with divine charity, that the outbidding of his soul would attract the attention of every observer. There was a very decided air, too, of the gentleman about Mr. Martyn, and a perfection of manners which, from his extreme attention to all minute civilities, might seem almost inconsistent with the general bent of his thoughts on the most serious subjects. He was as remarkable for ease as for cheerfulness.

A notice of Martyn by Sir John Malcolm, written a few years later, may be quoted appropriately here. He describes him to Sir Gore Ouseley, British Ambassador in Persia, as Martyn appeared at Bombay in 1811:

> The Rev. Mr. Martyn, one of the clergymen of Bengal, is here on his way to the Gulf. His knowledge of Arabic is superior to that of any Englishman in India. He is altogether a very learned and cheerful man, but a great enthusiast in his holy calling. He will give you grace before and after dinner, and admonish such of your party as take the Lord's name in vain; but his good sense and great learning will delight you, whilst his constant cheerfulness will add to the hilarity of your party.[1]

---

1. Life of Sir John Malcolm, ii. 65. Martyn himself, in a letter to Daniel Corrie,

At Cawnpore, finding himself well able to preach to the natives, Martyn regularly gathered a crowd of beggars round his bungalow door and spoke to them of Christ. What followed directly we do not know. But a noble indirect result was the conversion of a Mahometan gentleman, an official of the Court of Oude, one of a group who on these occasions listened only to deride. After Martyn's death he presented himself to Corrie for baptism, brought through the young Padre's remembered words to the feet of his Saviour. He exchanged a large income for a catechist's pay of sixty rupees a month; and in due time he received English orders. As his baptismal name he had chosen Abdul Messeeh, Bondman of Christ. I have in my keeping a miniature of his face, painted by a native artist, at Agra, for Simeon.[2] He was Martyn's one Indian convert; and Martyn never knew him.[3]

At Cawnpore the signs of inherited consumption began to tell upon the frail and always toiling man. He was to have come home on furlough, but the translator's and evangelist's ardour determined him instead to go on leave to Persia, there to improve to the utmost his Persian New Testament, which had been criticised at Calcutta. Its faults were not all Martyn's, but due very much to unfaithful and pedantic work by his blindly trusted munshi, Sabat, mistaken by Martyn for a true convert. He preached a last sermon at Cawnpore, 'beginning with a feeble voice, but gathering strength as he proceeded,

---

unconsciously indicates a beautiful feature in his own character, his affinity for children. He writes November 1, 1810: 'Came to Aldeen' (David Brown's home) 'at sunset – the children jumping, shouting, and convoying me in troops to the house' (Journals and Letters).

2. And brought to him 'by little James Thomason' in 1814. See pages 118-119 ....

3. There is a notice of Abdul Messeeh in Bishop Heber's Indian Journal (January 11, 1825), from which I have gathered most of the few particulars given here. Heber met him at Agra, and was greatly struck by his noble Christian character. He died in 1827.

till he seemed like one inspired from on high', and then went
down the river to Calcutta. There he met Thomason, lately
come also from Cambridge and from Trinity Church. 'He is
on his way to Arabia,' Thomason wrote to Simeon; 'you know
his genius, and what gigantic strides he takes in everything.
He has some great plan in his head of which I am no competent
judge; but so far as I do understand it, the object is too great
for one short life.'

About Easter, 1811, he arrived in Persia, at Bushire, and
soon settled at Shiraz, the learned city. Here he read and
translated, and invited and accepted discussion with the
mullahs. Often, and by some always, he was treated with
respect as a learned Frank and a man unmistakably holy.
One day, alone among the Moslem doctors, challenged to say
what was his belief about Christ, he solemnly confessed the
Godhead of his Lord. 'Was He the Creator, or a creature?' I
replied, 'The Creator ...' Such a confession had never before
been heard among them. 'You deserve to have your tongue
burnt out for this,' they said on another similar occasion. He
writes that he feels unworthy of the honour of their disgust,
'and of the brickbats which the boys throw at me'.

In Sir Gore Ouseley, the ambassador at Ispahan, he found
a sincere friend, and was allowed through his introduction to
present his translation to the Shah.

All this while the man who was thus always at work, and
always shedding from his life the pure unearthly brightness
of his Master's presence, carried about a heart faint with
disappointed human love. In his Cambridge days he had won
the heart of a lady worthy of even him, Lydia Grenfell. She
was the daughter of an old Cornish house, of which the next
generation, from one family, gave wives to Charles Kingsley
and James Anthony Froude. One of the most pathetic pages

of Martyn's brief history is his parting from Lydia Grenfell at
Gurlyn on August 10, 1805; when, as he was ministering at
family worship to her and her mother, a messenger led a horse
to the door, and summoned him instantly to St. Hilary and to
Falmouth, for the unexpected sailing of the fleet. In letters
scattered over his Memoir, and over its now scarce companion, his *Journals and Letters*, and, I may add, in some unpublished letters now by me, there is ample enough to show
how this intense and high affection went with him all through
his Indian and Persian labours. It was never to be consum-
mated. Miss Grenfell loved him, but she did not go out to
him; for reasons not now fully known, but certainly not of her
own making. The farewell at Gurlyn was the last embrace.
She long survived him, saintly, grave, always in earnest, 'gentle to others, to herself severe'; and she never married.

In 1812 it seemed as if it might be otherwise. He had been
ill almost to death, at Tebriz, while Sir Gore and Lady Ouseley
nursed him as a son. Recovering, he felt the thought of England
and of Lydia come strongly over him; he would return by
Constantinople, and bring her back to India and to his beloved
work. The leave was given, and the coming announced to
Simeon, and to her; and on September 2 he set out on
horseback, accompanied only by eastern servants. One of them,
'the merciless Hassan', was in some sense in command of
the party, and hurried Martyn beyond his little strength. They
reached Tocat in Asia Minor, seventy miles south of the Black
Sea, the place of Chrysostom's death fifteen centuries before;
and at Tocat, October 16, 1812, 'either falling a sacrifice to
the plague which then raged there, or sinking under that
disorder which had so greatly reduced him, he surrendered
his soul into the hands of his Redeemer', at the age of thirty-
one.

Over his grave, in 1813, a stone was placed by the English resident at Bagdad, Claudius Rich. But the spot was exposed to insult; and the coffin was at last removed to the garden of the American Mission, where an obelisk now marks the site, inscribed in four languages. A few particulars of Martyn's end were gleaned at Tocat, by the missionaries, in 1830. He probably died at the post-house, cared for in some measure by Armenian Christians, and Hassan took his portmanteau to Constantinople. In the portmanteau was found, among other things, his Diary, with its last entry, written ten days before his death:

> *Oct. 6th.* No horses being to be had, I had an unexpected repose. I sat in the orchard, and thought with sweet comfort and peace of my God, in solitude my company, my friend, and comforter. Oh! when shall time give place to eternity? When shall appear that new heavens and new earth wherein dwelleth righteousness? There, there shall in no wise enter anything that defileth; none of that wickedness which has made men worse than wild beasts, none of those corruptions which add still more to the miseries of mortality, shall be seen or heard of any more.
>
> My plans of seclusion in the woods at Lamorran have proved visionary. Till yesterday, when I sat for some hours on a moss-grown rock, incessant invitations from my friends have kept me in constant motion. The places near Lamorran are very favourable for meditation, as I hear no sound but the whistling of the curlew and the rippling of the waves. But these scenes are passing away, and I from them. And let them pass. Vanity is written on everything under the sun. The time is hastening when we shall forget the creature entirely, and be swallowed up in the love of God.

Martyn has been called 'the one heroic name which adorns the annals of the Church of England from the days of Elizabeth to our own'. This is not so, assuredly; but it is true that Martyn shines with a peculiar lustre in the catalogue of our

saints and confessors; a man at once eminently holy and truly
human, beautiful in the whole tone of his developed character, given up to the will and work of God with an unpretending
but entire surrender, and bending all the powers of a rare
intellect upon the 'one thing he did'. As regards mental calibre, it is certain that he was very much more than the extremely clever college competitor. Those who have a right to
speak have assured me that Martyn's linguistic work in
Hindustani, the one language which he had time really to master, is the work of a philological genius, and that everything
recorded of his missionary plans shows us a lofty and far-
reaching mind.

His best-known portrait confirms the impression of intellectual greatness. It is the picture sent from Calcutta, in 1812,
to Simeon, who, in a letter, describes its arrival, and how it
was unpacked at the India House:

> I could not bear to look upon it, but turned away, covering my face,
> and, in spite of every effort to the contrary, crying aloud with an-
> guish. E was with me, and all the bystanders said to her, 'That, I
> suppose, is his father.... Shall I attempt to describe to you the ven-
> eration and the love with which I look at it?... In seeing how much he
> is worn, I am constrained to call to my relief the thought in Whose
> service he has worn himself so much; and this reconciles me to the
> idea of weakness, of sickness, or even, if God were so to appoint,
> of death itself.... I behold in it all the mind of my beloved brother.'

As those words were written, Martyn was dying at Tocat.

The portrait was hung in Simeon's dining-room, over the
fire-place. He used often to look at it in his friends' presence, and to say, as he did so, with a peculiar loving emphasis, 'There, see that blessed man! What an expression of
countenance! No one looks at me as he does; he never takes
his eyes off me, and seems always to be saying, "Be serious

– be in earnest – don't trifle – don't trifle."' Then smiling at
the picture, and gently bowing, he would add, 'And I won't
trifle – I won't trifle.'

At the Church Missionary House is preserved a much earlier portrait. It shows the same face, but wearing an expression of almost boyish cheerfulness. I have in my charge a
miniature, taken for Simeon just before Martyn left England;
it has the younger look, but the shadows of toil and sorrow
are just coming over it. The Calcutta portrait was placed, at
Simeon's bequest, in the vestibule of the University Library.

Martyn's memory is ever-green in the hearts of English
Christians. Many years ago I heard, and I still hear them, the
thunders of applause with which his name was greeted from
the galleries when, in the Senate House, at a great University
meeting held in support of Livingstone's African work, the
late Bishop Wilberforce pronounced it in a passage of glowing eloquence. It is as familiar and as potent among us at this
day. And now it is materially commemorated in the beautiful
'Martyn Memorial Hall', raised, in 1887, close to Trinity
Church. Over the door of the Hall is placed an inscription,
written by the Master of the Temple, Dr. C.J. Vaughan: 'To
the inspiring memory of Henry Martyn, Scholar, Evangelist,
Confessor, and Man of God, a later generation of his own
Cambridge dedicates this home of Christian converse and
counsel.'

Thomas Thomason

In the chancel of Trinity Church, above the tablet which
Simeon placed there to Martyn's memory, the visitor sees
another like it, bearing the name of Thomas Thomason, and
'erected by his affectionate mother, E. Dornford'. Thomason
has been mentioned already as one of Simeon's early disci-

ples and friends. He entered Magdelene in 1792, and was the fifth Wrangler of 1796. From Magdalene he was invited to a Fellowship at Queens, and afterwards made Tutor there. In the year of his degree he was ordained, and served as a curate under Simeon till 1808, when he sailed for India. The friendship of the two men ripened into an endeared intimacy, and Thomason stood scarcely second to Martyn in Simeon's heart. Nothing could be happier than their relations in the duties of the church. Thomason, with very considerable ability, was a tranquil but indefatigable worker in his ministry; and the two friends felt so strong together that Simeon in 1796 undertook the Curacy-in-charge of Stapleford, five miles away in the country, where Berridge had preached fifty years before; and they worked it as a sort of rural dependency of Trinity. At Shelford, close to Stapleford, Thomason lived in a pleasant house through whose large garden flowed the stream of the Granta. Here Simeon would sometimes stay with him, and in that retirement they loved to study, pray, and write together, going out from it to visit the poor people of Stapleford. Simeon, always practical, organised a little 'society' there as at Cambridge, and he also introduced straw-plaiting in the cottages, to the lasting benefit of the villagers.

In 1807 work had begun to tell severely upon him, and for several years he was an invalid to some degree; in particular, his power for public speaking was greatly reduced. Thomason was called to fill the large gaps left in the pulpit-work, and developed remarkable power as a preacher, with a style not precisely eloquent, but rich and full. Simeon returned from an enforced absence, and heard his curate preaching with a depth and power which struck him at once as remarkable and as new, and saw his great command over the congregation. Some incumbents perhaps would not have re-

joiced without reserve; but Simeon knew no poor jealousy.
'Now I see why I have been withdrawn,' he said; and gave
God thanks. But the happy partnership was soon afterwards
dissolved. Thomason felt within him a strong call to the heathen world, and Simeon bade him go. He said farewell, in
June, 1808, to his deeply sorrowing mother, Mrs. Dornford,
Simeon's faithful Cambridge friend; and Simeon actually
sailed with him some way down the Channel. When at last he
left the ship, he pursued Thomason at once with a letter, the
first of a long and loving series: 'The wind has changed;
were it to blow hard, you would be driven back again. Shall
I appear unkind if I were to say, I should be grieved to see
you? Though I would not for a great deal have lost the opportunity of parting with you as I did, I would not willingly pass
through it again; a few such scenes would speedily wear and
enfeeble my frame. Yet... I wish you not to be delayed on
your voyage.'

The voyage ended in December, with a narrow escape
from shipwreck in the Bay of Bengal. Thomason, with his
wife, was allowed to labour for God in India till 1827. Then
his wife's ill-health brought him home; she died on the voyage, and he, reaching England, undertook an English parish
in his solitude. But he could not rest away from India and his
translations. In 1828 he returned, resigning his church and
his pension. But he reached India only to leave it again, quite
broken down, and he died and was buried at Mauritius.
Thomason was an admirable Orientalist, a wise and strong
missionary, and a holy man.

His young son, James, was sent home, in 1814, to Simeon's care; and faithful care it was indeed. All the father came
out in this man who had deliberately and resolutely chosen
the then necessary celibacy of a Fellowship that he might the

better work for God at Cambridge. He met the ship in the Thames; he 'received the dear treasure', and set off for Cambridgeshire with him. He resolved to 'steer the medium between excess of care, and want of care. You may be assured we shall have a hundred eyes, whilst we shall seem to have only a dozen. Flannels will be ready to put on at a moment; but I think it better not to endanger the making him too tender.' He soon took him to a private school; and in due time watched over his course at Haileybury with wise while yearning care. Letters of practical counsel to Bishops (for they had began to consult Simeon), and answers to anxious inquiries about the deep things of God, are interspersed in the records of that time with eager words to this dear child of his heart: 'My beloved James, I have this moment' (Nov. 6, 1821) 'received a letter which greatly afflicts me; it is the monthly report, in which the word "quite" is omitted, and even the word "very" is omitted, and nothing is said but "regular and correct".... Measure not your good behaviour by drams and scruples, but let the measure be full, pressed down, and running over. Tell me, my beloved James, by an early post, that you are determined, by God's help, that if I open the next report with fear, I shall read it with joy. This will be a great comfort to the mind of your loving father in man's stead, and your anxious father in God's stead, C. SIMEON.'

In the same year James Thomason returned to India; the future masterly Lieutenant-Governor of the North-West, a Christian ruler worthy of both his fathers; the guide of other civilians, afterwards themselves eminent, in the art of administering India for its inhabitants and for God.

Other friends

The space would fail me to tell the reader anything in detail of Simeon's other friends. Otherwise I might speak of Daniel Corrie, drawn to spiritual decision through Simeon's influence, and sent out by him to India in 1807, to labour as the bosom friend of Martyn, Thomason and Brown, and to die in 1837, worn out by his apostolic labours as first Bishop of Madras.

And of James Hough, the historian of Indian Christianity, and the second founder, after the Bohemian Lutheran Janicke, of the large and flourishing missions of Tinnevelly; ordained at Carlisle in 1815, and led to dedicate himself to India through an accidental interview with Simeon at Scaleby Castle in Cumberland.

And of Claudius Buchanan, the undutiful son of a Scottish schoolmaster, brought to the feet of Christ by a sermon of John Newton's preached in St. Mary Woolnoth; sent to Cambridge by Newton's friend, Henry Thornton; one of the little group who listened to Simeon's chamber readings on Revealed Religion; appointed to an East Indian chaplaincy in 1796, and for twelve years the laborious and able missionary student and teacher, and the earnest advocate of Indian missions in the English press.

Passing from the circle of 'Simeon's Chaplains', and touching that of his friends in general, I might describe Sowerby, the Senior Wrangler of 1798, at first strongly prejudiced against Trinity Church and its Minister; then persuaded to listen to a friend who offered to give him Scripture proof that his judgment was mistaken; then Thomason's colleague in Simeon's curacy; called early to rest, after a bright, devoted course.

I might dwell on the beautiful memory of Henry Kirke

White, the *protégé* of Robert Southey, welcomed to Cambridge
by Simeon and Martyn, but living only to begin his second
year. His academical promise was brilliant, and the poverty
of his family, much more than personal ambition, tempted
him to overwork a delicate constitution. He died, in his rooms,
at the age of twenty-one in October, 1806, having already
written his name on the roll of English Christian poets.

I might enlarge, with willing reverence, on the character
and work of James Scholefield, already named, Fellow of
Trinity College and (1825–1853) Regius Professor of Greek.
He was Simeon's curate for some years till 1823, and then
Vicar of St. Michael's till his death; an excellent Porsonian
scholar, and a still better Christian teacher, as he ministered
in his church to many undergraduate generations, showing
them by precept and example how to search and unfold the
Scriptures, and how to worship in spirit and truth.

The honoured name of Charles Clayton might claim a more
than passing mention; the active college tutor, and the untiring pastor and fruitful preacher (1851–1867) in Simeon's
place. There he was succeeded by another of Simeon's later
hearers and friends, Thomas Rawson Birks, second Wrangler of 1834, and in his latter days (1872–1883) Professor of
Moral Philosophy; an acute and indefatigable thinker, profound student of Scripture, and able teacher. And if I might
speak at large of the living, I should have much to write of
William Carus, Fellow and Dean of Trinity, Simeon's *mi
Carissime*, his friend, curate, biographer, and first successor
(1836–1851).

But this long chapter must end; and it shall end with an
extract in which a group of Simeon's earlier friends appear
together, in a picture of the Clerical Meetings of Shelford
and Aspeden.

The whole of the party, consisting sometimes of from twenty to thirty persons, were accommodated on the spot; and continued together two entire days, besides the days of arrival and departure. The clergy spent the mornings after breakfast in conference, principally on the Scriptures, Mr. Simeon presiding. A favourite book of his on these occasions was Warden's *System of Revealed Religion*, which contains a digest of Revelation under separate heads, composed in the express words of Scripture. The passages were usually read, first as collected together, and then separately, in the Old and New Testaments; copies of the original being continually consulted. These conferences, divested as much as possible of stiffness, which was the more easily effected from the harmony and mutual confidence of the brotherly circle, were exceedingly delightful. God, being thus enquired after in His own Word by those whose province it was to dispense it to others, the search after His will being begun and ended with prayer, did assuredly manifest Himself to them as He does not to the world. They have often said in words, and oftener in their hearts, 'It is good for us to be here.'

While the clergy were thus employed, the ladies were in another room, where they read together. At the hours of repast and in the evenings all met together. After tea there was usually some leading topic of conversation;... letters also, or any religious intelligence, or schemes of usefulness likely to be generally acceptable, were then brought forward.

This narrative will perhaps abate the fears of some persons who have apprehended they scarcely know what lurking mischief from such 'unauthorized assemblies'. If any such could have seen and heard without being seen, they would haply have fallen upon their knees and confessed that God was in that place. They would at least have witnessed there, what is recorded to have taken place in olden time; when 'they that feared the Lord spake often one to another; and the Lord hearkened, and heard it; and a book of remembrance was written before Him for them that feared the Lord, and thought upon His name'. Certainly not one of those who have been present at those seasons now repents – except of not having profited more from such opportunities. Never probably will some of them know more than they then experienced of the delight of the communion of saints, till they shall again meet with Martyn, and Jowett, and Lowe, and

Thomason, and Sargent, and Simeon, and Farish, and Daniel Wilson, and others whom we could name... in heaven.'

These meetings were continued till 1817.

Simeon himself writes after one such occasion, July 28, 1809: 'O for more of that divine composure, that tender love, that heavenly ardour, which animated the whole company.'

Chapter 10

Scotland

I have a great work before me, and much encouragement. Multitudes of gownsmen attend; prejudices wear away; the godly go on well. What can I wish for more to stimulate me? O that I had a mind to the work – such, I mean, as I ought to have! Then we might hope that the building would be carried up quicker. However, thanks be to God, though 'we are faint, we are yet pursuing'. I have had two young Scotch ministers to dine with me today. They brought a letter to me from Edinburgh; and I have had unspeakable cause for thankfulness that they did.

Simeon writes thus to a friend in 1795. My desultory narrative has often already carried me far beyond that date; I recur to it here chiefly for the sake of the last sentences of the extract. They bring us to the opening of one of the most interesting and important episodes of Simeon's life, his visits to Scotland and the influence which he exerted there.

England owes much to Scotland in the matter of Christian benefit. The country of Rutherford and of Leighton (the collection of those names is strange from the point of view of church organisation, deeply natural from that of spiritual life) has taught us of the south some of the inmost lessons of the school of grace. And what English Christian who has been moved and instructed by the words and work of Chalmers, the Bonars, Candlish, McCheyne or Hewitson, does not thank Scotland for such messengers to the Church? England on her part has been the minister of spiritual gifts to Scotland; and in his day Simeon was one of the chief agents of that ministry.

We do not know the names of the 'two young Scotch ministers' of 1795, nor who wrote their letter of introduction. But their visit probably led to Simeon's acquaintance in 1796 with an able and earnest clergyman in Edinburgh, William Buchanan, who visited Cambridge, and ·soon persuaded Simeon to take his annual holiday in Scotland. That year the friends went together to Edinburgh, and Simeon travelled through the Highlands. Again in 1798 he visited the far north with Buchanan, going to Inverness and Tain. Scotland was not then the familiar resort of holiday-taking Englishmen, as it has so long been now. The visitor made his way through many a district rarely traversed from outside, and his lodging was the village inn, when he was not the guest at mansion or manse. Simeon's favourite conveyance was his horse, which carried him far over the Highland roads and paths.

His holidays were not by any means cessations in his work for God. Wherever he went he appeared as the Christian and as the clergyman, ready for his Master's business as occasion offered. And the occasions were many, both for private intercourse and household devotion, and for public preaching, as the narrative will show.

This is not the place for a review of Scottish religious history. All that is necessary as a preface to Simeon's work in the north is to remind the reader that his first visits there fell about half-way between two important spiritual epochs in the Presbyterian Church. In the earlier half of the eighteenth century the too rigid order of Church life had been disturbed by a first and a second movement towards a fuller and heartier spiritual faith and witness; each movement issuing in a secession from the main body. The names of Ralph and Ebenezer Erskine and Thomas Gillespie mark that period. And seven years after Simeon's death occurred the great ecclesiastical crisis of 'the Disruption', when the Free Church

of Scotland was organised. Alike the earlier and the later
upheaval and separation may be viewed, of course, from very
different points. But it can hardly be denied of either that the
circumstances, however they were dealt with on any side,
were full to overflowing of true spiritual factors. A prevalent indifference or oblivion about the Christianity of Scripture was invaded by a revival of Scriptural truth and life; and
some sort of disturbance was inevitable, by no fault of the
invading principle in itself. I for one would fain believe that
in all such times of crisis in the Christian Church there might
well have been found, speaking humanly, some better way
than that of an outward dislocation, if both parties could have
acted with a single and watchful aim towards truth and peace.
But was there ever yet seen quite such action on both sides in
great practical controversies in the Church?

However, Simeon's first visits to Scotland fell between
the age of the earlier Secessions and that stirring time which
immediately preceded the rise of the Free Church. He found
accordingly around him, almost wherever he went, individual
instances of warm Christian life, much earnest pastoral labour, and some vigorous irregular efforts, and on the other
hand the cooler and too negative influence of a widely prevalent 'Moderatism'. It is remarkable that his admission to
Presbyterian pulpits, of which I shall soon come to speak,
was opposed not (so far as any hint appears) by High Churchmen in England but by the Moderates in the General Assembly of the Church of Scotland. The activity of 'the Itinerants', as some lay-evangelists were called, who had left the
Scottish Church for Congregationalism, and who had not always acted and spoken wisely, had alarmed and displeased
the Moderate leaders, and prepared them for an unfavourable view of Simeon's energetic preaching. His appearance

as a minister in parish churches had given a precedent for some similar ministrations by the Itinerants. And in 1799 the Assembly enacted, under strong protest from the Evangelicals (their opponents called them the Highfliers), 'that no preacher who is not a licentiate of, and no minister who has not been ordained by some Presbytery of the Church of Scotland shall ever officiate in any of its pulpits'. In his later visits to the North Simeon was thus debarred from parochial preaching.

In his private 'Memoir' he speaks thus of his ministrations in parish churches:

> I officiated precisely as they do in the Kirk of Scotland; and I did so upon this principle: Presbyterianism is as much the established religion in North Britain as Episcopacy is in the South, there being no difference between them, except in Church government. As an Episcopalian therefore I preached in Episcopal chapels, and as a member of the Established Church I preached in the Presbyterian churches; and I felt myself the more warranted to do this, because, if the King, who is head of the Establishment in both counties, were in Scotland, he would of necessity attend at a Presbyterian church there, as he does at an Episcopalian church here. And I look upon it as an incontrovertible position that where the King must attend a clergyman may preach. I was informed indeed that Archbishop Ussher had preached in the Kirk of Scotland, and I know that some very high churchmen had done so; but without laying any stress on precedents, I repeat that, where the King and his court must attend, a clergyman may preach.[1]

Some interesting details of this visit follow in Simeon's diary:

> *Sunday, 19th June, 1879.* Went with Messrs. Innes and Campbell to St. Ninian's (near Stirling). Mr. Sheriff began the service, and preached an useful sermon from Hebrews 10:10. After preaching

---

1. In a memorandum of 1822 he mentions with interest the fact that in that year George the Fourth had attended St. Giles'.

above an hour, besides prayer and singing, he left the pulpit and went to the head of the tables. There he gave us exhortation respecting the Sacrament, which to me was more excellent than his sermon.... I communicated at the second table, where Mr. Campbell exhorted. His exhortation was exceedingly precious to my soul; I was quite dissolved in tears; I made a free, full, and unreserved surrender of myself to God. O that I may ever bear in mind His kindness to me, and my obligations to Him! After communicating I left them, and saw, as I came into the churchyard, one preaching there in a tent. This preacher was Mr. C. of Bathcannor; I did not stop to hear him, lest I should lose the blessed frame in which my soul then was. I walked home alone by choice, and met numbers coming to the Sacrament, which, as I understood, lasted till about eight in the evening. They had about a thousand communicants – a fresh exhortation to every table, and a sermon to conclude.

But we must come without delay to the much more interesting and important incident of that northern tour: the English clergyman's visit to Moulin, and its results.

Influences the minister of Moulin

Moulin is the parish in which lies the now favourite and populous health-resort of Pitlochry, just at the southern gate of the Pass of Killiecrankie, in the noble Highlands of Perthshire. There the Tummel and the Garry, rushing each from its deep and leafy ravine, united their waters; and the visitor's thoughts are divided between the glories of nature and the traditions of that famous fight in 1689 when, in the broad field at the head of the Pass, the Highland host suddenly and totally overthrew the regiments of General McKay, just emerging with difficulty from the dark gorge, and John Graham of Claverhouse, Lord Dundee, fell in the moment of his triumph. But another and far different memory belongs also to the scenery, for those who love the annals of Christian life. Into this ro-

mantic region Simeon came riding, by way of Dunkeld, in his
first June in Scotland; and the parish Minister of Moulin was
Alexander Stewart, a man of beautiful character and some
considerable gifts and attainments. In his early manhood he
had attracted the attention and respect of Dugald Stewart by
some unpublished metaphysical papers, and he had also come
to be known as one of the best Gaelic scholars of his time;
his Gaelic grammar had a high reputation. He was a native of
that fine region, and warmly in love with its scenery and
associations, and he was the centre of a happy home. But his
soul was beclouded and uneasy. He preached a pure and high
morality, and he held in a certain sense the doctrines of Christian orthodoxy. But he saw no satisfying results of his labour
among his people, and he was himself restlessly conscious
that secrets of spiritual joy and power lay near him undis-
covered. Then it was that he met the English traveller. Simeon's diary makes a brief mention of the occasion:

Friday, 24th. Set out for Dunkeld; saw the Duke of Atholl's grounds.
Here I was fatigued with my walk; we declined prosecuting our journey, notwithstanding the horses were at the door. There, through
mercy, I slept sweetly, and pursued my journey on Saturday 25th to
Moulin; twelve miles in my way to Blair Atholl. At Moulin I visited
the Rev. Mr. Stewart, a most agreeable and pious man. The Sacrament was to be administered next day, and according to custom there
were two complete services; but the former alone was in English. I
heard the discourse from Mr. E., minister of Blair. He is an old
man, and wants life and animation. Neither myself nor Mr. H.[1] was
much edified. After the service we went to Blair. We returned through
Killiecrankie Pass to Moulin.

---

1. James Haldane, afterwards resident at Geneva, whre he was the means of
spiritual awakening to J.H. Merle d'Aubigne, Cesar Malan, A. Gaussen, and many
other students of the University.

Sunday, 26th. Sacrament Sunday at Moulin. The congregation was numerous, and the communicants almost a thousand. I preached a short sermon, and while they were partaking, I spoke a few words of encouragement, and bid them depart in peace. I expressed to them in the former exhortation my fears respecting the formality which obtains among all the people, and urged them to devote themselves truly to Jesus Christ. After that I partook with the third table. On the whole this Sabbath was not like the last. Then I was very much affected; now I was barren and dull. God, however, is the same, and His word is unchangeable; and in that is all my hope. Woe be to me if I were to be saved by my frames; nevertheless, I would never willingly be in a bad one. At six in the evening I preached again to those who understood English; but they were few, and they seemed not to understand me. In the evening Mr Stewart came up into my room; and we had much useful conversation about the ministry. He complained of unprofitableness, and was much affected during the conversation. We prayed together, and parted very affectionately, with the *osculum pacis*. He promised to write to me.

That memorable day and night, for it was such for Stewart, and through him for many other lives, is recorded more fully in Simeon's private 'Memoir':

When I was in the Highlands, it was my intention to go as far as the pass of Killiecrankie, and afterwards return to Dunkeld, on a Friday afternoon. But at Dunkeld I found myself poorly; and when my horses were brought to the door, I ordered them back, and proceeded to Killiecrankie the next day. At Moulin, a village four miles from Killiecrankie, I called to see a Mr. Stewart, to whom I had a letter of introduction; and as it was the day of preparation for the Lord's Supper, which in Scotland is observed with peculiar solemnity and long public services, I agreed to visit the pass of Killiecrankie, and return for his services and spend the Sabbath with him. Mr Stewart was a man in high repute both for amiableness of manners and for learning; but he was very defective in his views of the Gospel and his experience of its power. When we were all retiring to go to bed, I had him with me alone in my chamber, and spoke such things as occurred to my mind with a view to his spiritual good; and it pleased

God so to apply them to his heart that they were made effectual for the opening of his eyes and bringing him into the marvellous light of the Gospel of Christ. From that moment he changed the strain of his preaching, determining to know nothing among his people but Jesus Christ and Him crucified; and God has now, for these fifteen years, made his instructions most eminently useful for the conversion and salvation of many souls.

One name, ever to be famous in the annals of Christian missions, is nearly though indirectly connected with that day. The late Dr. Duff, of Calcutta, the prince of missionary educationists, was the son of parishioners of Stewart's. The parents 'owed their own selves' to the now transfigured matter and tone of their Minister's teaching. They brought up their child in the full faith of the Gospel, and with a special dedication of his life to the service of Christ. A bronze statue of the great Missionary now stands close to one of the churches in Pitlochry; and to those who know the story of Simeon and Stewart it is a monument also to them.

As we might suppose, the two men thus brought together in Christ found themselves at once the dearest of intimates. Simeon's strong and eager heart was opened to Stewart without reserve, and Stewart responded with all the tender warmth which so often lies beneath the more reticent surface of the northern character. Let me quote a few sentences from one of his letters to his now beloved friend:

Moulin, November 25, 1796.
Ever since the few happy hours in which I was blessed with your company, I have daily thought, with pleasure and gratitude, of the Lord's lovingkindness to me in sending two of His chosen servants, so unexpectedly and so seasonably, to speak to me the words of life.... My kind friend Mr. Haldane, in a letter received two days ago, tells me you have not forgotten me, and that you desire to hear from me. I wish I knew how to express my filial regard and attach-

ment to one whom I have every reason to consider as my spiritual father. If Onesimus might call Paul his father, with the like reason may I call Mr. Simeon mine. For indeed I found from your conversation, your prayers, preaching, and particularly from our short interview in your bedroom, more of religious impression and more of spiritual life and ardour infused into my soul than ever I was conscious of before.... O my dear Sir, praise the Lord on my behalf who hath given me to perceive something of His glory and His grace as displayed in Christ Jesus; though I have a great deal yet to see and to learn.... In emulation of your manner of preaching, I have for four months past preached English from short skeletons, without reading, or committing to memory; a thing I had never attempted before. My discourse is less correct, and must offend a critic; but it is more energetic, and may profit a soul that is hungry for the bread of life.... Grace and peace be with you.

> Yours most sincerely,
> Alex. Stewart.

P.S. – A poor woman in this village, who heard you preach here, insists on my letting you know how much she enjoyed your discourse, and how much she was revived by it. She lives quite alone, in a small hovel, on a scanty provision; yet she enjoys a great measure of the Lord's countenance, and lives much in communion with Him.... Do, my dear Sir, remember me in your prayers. In mine, such as they are, I seldom omit making mention of you.

Simeon replies at once to his 'very, very dear friend':

There is an unaccountable union of heart with, or, if I may so express myself, an outgoing of the soul toward, some persons which we feel instantaneously and we know not why. Such I felt almost the first instant I saw my dear friend at Moulin. I hope it is an earnest of that everlasting union which our souls shall enjoy in the regions of light and love.... I am exceedingly comforted, my dear brother, with the account which you give of your soul. O how desirable is it for all, but especially for ministers, to have their souls deeply and devoutly impressed! I pray God that what you now experience may only be as the drop before the shower. Surely this is happiness, to

taste the love of God, to find delight in His service, and to see that
we are in a measure instrumental to the imparting of this happiness
to others, – this, I say, is a felicity which nothing but heaven can
exceed.... The account you give of the dear poor woman rejoices
my heart.... Pray give my fervent love to her.

Stewart's life was henceforth full of fruitful labours. A
few years later than Simeon's visit there came over Moulin
and its neighbourhood one of those times of religious awakening which seem like after-waves of the first Pentecost. It
was directly due, under God, to the Minister's altered preaching and untiring pastoral diligence. And his own character
seemed to mould the movement; there was abundant repentance in the many converts, and a chastened happiness, and a
remarkable amendment of morals in the whole neighbourhood, but an almost total absence of even the look of un-
wholesome excitement.

In 1805, Stewart was made Minister of the town of Ding-
wall, in Ross-shire; and there laboured in a very different
field, equally displaying firmness in reproving and opposing
vice and affectionate gentleness in temper and manner. In 1820,
he was unexpectedly presented by the Crown to the 'First
Charge' of Canongate parish, in Edinburgh. But his work there
was very short. An old malady returned upon him, and he
died in 1821, beloved and long lamented.[1]

Simeon left Moulin soon after that Sunday:

Thursday, 30th. To Ben Lomond. From the foot we arrived at the
top in three hours. Mr. H. and myself then went to prayer, and dedi-
cated ourselves afresh to God. We then surveyed the scenery, which

1. My authority is an anonymous *Memoir of Dr. Alexander Stewart*. The copy I
have consulted belongs to Canon Carus; it was Simeon's, and on the flyleaf he has
written: The gift of my ever dear and honoured friend, Dr. Buchanan, November 8,
1822.

to the north-west was exceedingly grand; for immediately across
the lake were a vast multitude of hills, whose lofty summits, clad in
russet, formed a view totally different from anything I had ever seen.
We had a bird's-eye view of them, and their appearance was inex-
pressibly majestic.

That view of the great Loch with its many islands gave him a
vivid simile, used long afterwards. Seen from the water the
islands were large and broken masses; seen from the moun-
tain they lay 'flat as pancakes' in the distance. So may some
of the differences which now separate Christians sink into an
almost nothing when seen from the point of view of the eternal state.

The tour of 1796 was followed by others in 1798, 1815
and 1819. This last occasion was the visit noticed above,
when Simeon went with his friend Marsh as an advocate of
the cause of Jewish missions.

Simeon's intercourse with Scottish Christians did much
to bring about a better mutual understanding between them
and their English brethren. It was a surprise to many in the
north to see a southern clergyman mount the pulpit with only
his little Bible in his hand, and preach with the utmost freedom
and energy, yet with exactness of diction and a clear order of
thought. And Simeon on his part was evidently impressed by
the presence around him in Scotland of the tokens of deep
spiritual life and of diligent pastoral labour.

His loyalty to the English Church and its worship was by
no means shaken meantime. The Prayer-book, always dear
to him, grew dearer as he returned again to its use. Extem-
porary public prayer he could and did approve in theory, and
often in experience. But he found that *average* conditions
were much better met by an ordered form, reverently and
spiritually used.

I cannot help recording here, to the honour of the Church of England, that on all the three times that I have visited Scotland, and have attended almost entirely the Presbyterian churches, I have on my return to the use of our Liturgy.... felt it an inestimable privilege that we possess a form of sound words, so adapted in every respect to the wants and desires of all who would worship God in spirit and in truth.

If *all* men could pray at all times as *some* men can *sometimes*, then indeed we might prefer extempore to pre-composed prayers.

Chapter 11

Work in Weakness

It is time to return to Simeon's life and labour at Cambridge. We have followed him in his interests to India, and in his person to Scotland. But his diligence at home never knew any willing remission from the first to the last.

There was indeed a long time during which his strength was reduced so much as to lessen his public activity, and even to keep him absent from Cambridge for many months. Early in 1807, after twenty-five years of intense work, in which Thornton's cautions had been too often forgotten, he felt his health fail; and particularly his voice became so weak that he could preach only with difficulty and never more than once in the day. After each sermon he found himself 'more like one dead than alive', and even conversation was often impossible, unless in a whisper.

This broken condition lasted with variations for thirteen years, till he was just sixty, and then it passed away quite suddenly and without any evident physical cause. He was on his last visit to Scotland, with Marsh in 1819, and found himself to his great surprise, just as he crossed the Border, 'almost as perceptibly renewed in strength as the woman was after she had touched the hem of our Lord's garment'. He saw in this revival no miracle, in the common sense of the word, yet a distinct providence. He says that he had been promising himself, before he began to break down, a very active life up to sixty, and then a Sabbath evening; and that now he seemed to hear his Master saying: 'I laid you aside,

because you entertained with satisfaction the thought of rest-
ing from your labour; but now you have arrived at the very
period when you had promised yourself that satisfaction, and
have determined instead to spend your strength for me to the
latest hour of your life, I have doubled, trebled, quadrupled
your strength, that you may execute your desire on a more
extended plan.' 'I do not approve,' he says, as he looks back
in 1820, 'of fancying myself more an object of God's special
care and favour than other people, and much less of recording any such conceit; but this particular interposition of the
divine goodness I think I ought to see and acknowledge.'

Yet these years of comparative weakness were years of
much and varied work. The reader may remember that some
of the most important incidents given in previous chapters
fell within that time. He preached several courses at the
University Church (1810, 1811, 1815), on subjects which
drew great attention, with a vigour which entirely concealed
the effort which it cost. So great was the crowd in 1811 that
many Masters of Arts were driven into the galleries to find
room. The sermons of 1810, 'Evangelical and Pharisaic
Righteousness Compared', drew him into a controversy of
letters and pamphlets with the Master of Sidney, Edward
Pearson, who charged him with setting up an impossible
standard of holiness, and applying it uncharitably to his neighbours. Both Pearson and Simeon (who had a wise counsellor in Farish, from whom he learnt how to keep sarcasm and
ridicule quite out of his replies) show well in this paper war,
as regards mutual courtesy and the wish to be fair. Pearson
incidentally speaks of Simeon with hearty respect; and Simeon's last letter to Pearson (March, 1810) is worthy of quotation:

MY DEAR SIR,

Permit me to return you my best thanks for the present of your 'Remarks'; and to say that I most cordially agree with you in terminating our public correspondence. I am persuaded that, if circumstances should ever bring us into a nearer acquaintance with each other, we should find that the difference between us, though certainly great, is not so great as may at first sight appear. Persons who have the same general design, but differ in some particular modes of carrying it into execution, often stand more aloof from each other than they do from persons whose principles and conduct they entirely disapprove. Hence prejudice arises and a tendency to mutual crimination; whereas, if they occasionally conversed for half an hour with each other, they would soon rectify their mutual misapprehensions, and concur in aiding, rather than undermining the efforts of each other for the public good. The number of those who are zealous in the cause of religion is not so great but that they may find ample scope for their exertions without wasting their time in mutual contentions; and it is my earnest wish that the only strife we may ever know in future may be that which the Apostles recommend, of 'contending earnestly for the faith once delivered to the saints', and of 'provoking one another to love, and to good works'.

With these sentiments and wishes, I beg leave to subscribe myself,
Dear Sir, with great respect and esteem,
Your most obedient Servant,
C. SIMEON.

About the same time Simeon had to deal with the anxious crisis of the Bible Society's meeting, already described; and a little later came the last serious difficulties caused by opponents within his parish, trials which so oppressed him at the time that he writes to a friend, in 1812, 'I used to sail in the Pacific; I am now learning to navigate the Red Sea, that is full of shoals and rocks.' But the troubled period was not long. 1817 saw the last of it; and a year earlier he speaks of his church as better attended than ever, and sometimes half filled with undergraduates.

Social trials, however, were not over by any means. He writes to Thomason, March, 1816, and alludes to one of these:

> I have at this moment sweet consolation from the thought that God will ultimately be glorified in men, whether they will or not. Such conduct is observed towards me at this very hour by one of the Fellows of the College as, if practised by me, would set not the College only but the whole town and University in a flame. But the peace and joy which I experience, from lying as clay in the Potter's hands, are more than I can express. I forbear to state particulars; but I know that, whether man give or take away, it is not man but the Lord; and that 'He doeth all things well', and that, if we only wait to the end, we shall see infallible wisdom and unbounded goodness in His darkest dispensations. The example of our blessed Lord, who, without either threatening or complaint, 'committed himself to Him that judgeth righteously', appears to me most lovely; and I have unspeakable delight in striving (and hitherto with some success) to tread in His steps. God has long taught you this lesson, and I am endeavouring to learn it day by day. A little of the δοκιμη will be an ample compensation for a good deal of θλιψις.

In 1814, his brother Edward Simeon died in the Isle of Wight, after a long and painful illness. All the old prejudices against his brother's 'enthusiasm' were gone long before the end, and Charles had the great happiness of seeing Edward, the upright and successful man of business, welcome 'the common salvation' with great simplicity and joy, and at last depart in peace. Before he died, he pressed his brother, in the warmth of loving gratitude, to accept the half of his large property. But the earnest wish was in vain. To yield to it would have compelled Charles, as a matter of honour, to resign his Fellowship, and it would probably have made it his duty to leave Cambridge. He was certain that Cambridge and his position at King's were God's order for him; and nothing was to be allowed to move him. But he accepted a bequest of £15,000; how, and with what a purpose, his own words shall tell:

Memorandum.

K.C., Cambridge.

Last week I returned from Bristol, where I witnessed a thing almost unprecedented in the annals of the world, – a whole city combining to fill up by their united exertions the void made in all charitable Institutions by the loss of one man, Richard Reynolds, a member of the Society called Quakers. Having myself acted in some measure upon that idea, in relation to my dear and honoured brother, Edward Simeon, I take this opportunity of recording it for the satisfaction of myself and my executors.

My brother was extremely liberal, and did good to a vast extent. At his death an exceeding great void would have been made, if I had not determined to accept a part of his property and to appropriate it to the Lord's service and the service of the poor. The loss they would have sustained being about £700 or £800 a year, I suffered my brother to leave me £15,000, and have regularly consecrated the interest of it to the Lord; and shall (D.V.) continue to do so to my dying hour. Had I wished for money for my own use, I might have had half his fortune; but I wanted nothing for myself, being determined (as far as such a thing could be at any time said to be determined) to live and die in College, where the income which I previously enjoyed (though moderate in itself) sufficed not only for all my own wants, but for liberal supplies to the poor also.

These things are well known at present in our College (Mr. – in particular, as a counsel, examined my brother's will, wherein there is proof sufficient of these things); but at a future period they may be forgotten, and persons may wonder that, with my income, I do not resign my Fellowship. The fact is, I have not increased my own expenditure above £50 a year; nor do I consider myself as anything but a steward of my deceased brother for the poor.... Long previous to his death, I refused what was considered as the best living of our College; and I should equally refuse anything that the King himself could offer me that should necessitate me to give up my present situation, and especially my church. And I write this now, that if, after my decease, it should be asked, 'Why did he not vacate his Fellowship?' my executor may have a satisfactory answer at hand. It lies in a short space:

1st. If twice £15,000 were offered me to vacate my Fellowship, I would reject it utterly.

2nd. The legacy I have received I do not consider as mine, but as belonging to the poor and to the Lord; and I am only the steward, to whose hands it is committed.

3rd. The proof of this will be found in my refusal of any living before, as well as since, my brother's death, and in my account-books, wherein the disposal of this money is regularly entered.

Witness my hand this 19th of October, 1816.

Certainly he was consistent in a noble indifference to money. It was no easy-going carelessness. He once gave £20 to an accountant as a fee for the detection of a puzzling mistake of one penny in his private accounts. But gain, for its own sake, was as dust beneath his feet.

Simeon's sense of the extreme importance and awful responsibility of the work of Church patronage was deep and practical. He had no objection on principle to our certainly anomalous system; but he felt that it cries aloud for conscientious and religious care, if it is to work good at all. And a plan presented itself early to his mind; he would acquire by purchase the patronage of such livings as he could, and commit to trustees who should be men of fidelity and prayer. His enterprise (for which Henry Thornton had given a precedent) soon drew the attention of men who knew and trusted him, and who could either give him funds for purchase, or make over their own patronage into his hands. So grew up the Simeon Trust, which now has to do with a large number of English parishes. Most solemn is Simeon's 'charge' to his trustees – to take care that nothing comes first in their reasons for selection but the glory of God and the fitness of the particular man for the parish in question.

Chapter 12

Meetings for Undergraduates

Simeon's diligence as a pastor and preacher was the main foundation of his religious influence, and with this must be remembered his activity as a writer, and the very large circulation of his published Sermons and Outlines. But his work for religion in the University and in the English Church was carried into detail, and personally applied, in his informal meetings for undergraduates more than in any other way. We have seen how early he took up this line of work, in his small sermon-parties and private lectures on religion. To the last these labours were maintained, and the numbers of men who entered his rooms continually grew.

It may be interesting to describe the place of such gatherings: his abode in the Fellows' Building at King's College. From 1782 to 1812 he occupied, as I have said above, a set of rooms on the ground floor in that building. In 1812 he removed to a larger set, where he remained till his death, four-and-twenty years; and those rooms saw his most numerous gatherings for instruction and conversation.

The visitor who enters King's College from the front sees opposite to him the stately length of the Fellows' Building, now a hundred and sixty years old. It is broken midway by a lofty arch, through which the great lawn is seen and the trees of 'the Backs'; and over this arch appears a large semi-circular window. This window lights the front room, or dining-room, of the set which was Simeon's. Another large room, which he called his drawing-room, looks the other way, westward, through two sash-windows. The bedroom adjoins the dining-room, and out of it a steep staircase leads to a spacious attic in the roof. From the attic again there is an exit, through a glass door out upon the leads, where one may walk either along the edge of the building, just within the stone balustrade, or in the long hollow between the two ridges of the roof.

The rooms are approached by a staircase opening just north of the large archway. An iron handrail is carried up that staircase to the door of Simeon's rooms; it was placed there in his old age, to assist him on the long ascent, and is still called *The Saint's Rest!* The main door of the suite, guarded by the 'sporting-oak', opens on a passage running across the building and leading into the drawing-room. Out of this passage another goes leftwards into the dining-room, past the bedroom. Both passages are lined with a long row of hat-pegs, evidently put there by Simeon for the comfort of his many guests. And another characteristic attention he paid to them, and to his carpets, was to furnish the upper landing with a *scraper*, and to lay along the two passages a series of many door-mats, so that the yellow gravel of the court might be effectually rubbed off before the parlour floor was trodden. Always neat and careful, he 'loved a nice clean carpet'; and when sometimes a visitor, thoughtless or deep in thought, had forgotten to use the mats in time, he would take him back to the door to do his duty. There is a story of his behaving thus even to Henry Martyn; of course in the ground-floor rooms of his earlier days. Martyn, in his warmth of heart, had walked straight from the London coach to greet Simeon, bringing in with him a muddy pair of boots; and Simeon clasped 'his beloved brother by the hands – but in the same act drew him to the mat'.

The two chief rooms are the ideal of their kind; large and lofty, and abundantly light. The dining-room faces the morning sun, and a certain chair opposite its great window was a favourite place with Simeon in the early hours. When he first occupied the set this room looked out to the left upon the giant buttresses of the Chapel close by, and beyond them to the spire of Trinity Church, visible above the intervening roofs; and in front, in those days, it commanded the trees and the old houses which disappeared in 1824 to give way to the present Screen. The drawing-room is one of the most charming rooms in the University, looking out on the lawn, and the river, and the little forest of elms beyond, through windows which receive the full brightness of the West. The informal meetings were usually held in the drawing-room, and there also much of Simeon's private work was done, as he sat on a little leathern sofa, which is still preserved and still used; it was given by Canon Carus to Ridley Hall some years ago. Beside it in my study stands a massive mahogany armchair, also long used by Simeon; given to me by Mr. Clayton, of Cambridge, on the death of Canon Clayton, his brother. This, however, was not Simeon's throne on Friday evenings; he sat then on a large mahogany stool without arms or back.

But let me not forget the passage from the attic to the roof. This was a chief attraction in Simeon's eyes, when the choice of the set of rooms came to his turn. 'I shall now have a solitary oratory on the roof, where no eye but that of the Supreme can behold me.' Here he could walk up and down in the open air, yet at home and quite in secret, and so hold communion with God in prayer. On that high place, for the Fellows' Building is so lofty that even the Chapel-roof looks near when seen from it, there is a great feeling of freedom and quiet, and the path along the top between the ridges is

quite invisible save from the Chapel. An attic window, lighting other rooms, opens upon the path, but in Simeon's time
this was never used; and the old man's heavenly Master alone
can tell how often he paced that narrow way, confessing,
petitioning, consulting, praising, adoring. If I do not mistake,
those leads were often wet with his tears, and often pressed
with his knees as he paused for some special act of worship;
for no man ever felt more deeply than Simeon did the blessedness and the duty of adoration. He loved to speak of that
great vision of the prophet, where the six-winged Seraphim
'fly with twain, but with four wings veil themselves before
the eternal glory'. I pause, as it were upon the roof which
was his oratory, to quote an extract or two from words of his
upon the spirit of worship:

> It is doubtless a most joyful thought that we have redemption through
> the blood of our adorable Saviour. But I have no less comfort in the
> thought that He is exalted to give *repentance* and remission of sins.
> I would not wish for the latter without the former. I scarcely ask for
> the latter in comparison of the former. I feel willing to leave the
> latter altogether in God's hands if I may but obtain the former. Re-
> pentance is in every view so desirable, so necessary, so suited to
> honour God, that I seek that above all. The tender heart, the broken
> and contrite spirit, are to me far above all the joys I could ever hope
> for in this vale of tears. I long to be in my proper place, my hand on
> my mouth, and my mouth in the dust. I would rather have my seed-
> time here, and wait for my harvest till I myself am carried to the
> granary of heaven. I feel this to be safe ground. Here I cannot err ....
> I am sure that whatever God may despise (and I fear that there is
> much which passes under the notion of religious experience that
> will not stand very high in His estimation), He will not despise the
> broken and contrite heart. I love the picture of the heavenly hosts,
> both saints and angels; all of them are upon their faces before the
> throne.

And again:

> This is the religion that pervades the whole Liturgy, and particularly
> the Communion Service; and this makes the Liturgy inexpressibly
> sweet to me. The repeated cries to each Person of the ever-ador-
> able Trinity for mercy are not at all too frequent or too fervent for
> me; nor is the confession in the Communion service too strong for
> me; nor the *Te Deum*, nor the ascriptions of glory after the Lord's
> Supper, 'Glory be to God on high,' etc., too exalted for me; the
> praise all through savours of adoration, and the adoration of humil-
> ity. And this shows what men of God the framers of our Liturgy
> were, and what I pant, and long, and strive to be. This makes the
> Liturgy as superior to all modern compositions as the work of a
> philosopher on any deep subject is to that of a schoolboy who un-
> derstands scarcely anything about it ....
>
> The consequence of this unremitted labour is that I have, and
> have continually had, such a sense of my sinfulness as would sink
> me into utter despair, if I had not an assured view of the sufficiency
> and willingness of Christ to save me to the uttermost. And at the
> same time I had such a sense of my acceptance through Christ as
> would overset my little bark, if I had not ballast at the bottom suffi-
> cient to sink a vessel of no ordinary size. This experience has been
> now so unintermitted for forty years, that a thought only of some
> defect, or of something which might have been done better, often
> draws from me as deep a sigh as if I had committed the most enor-
> mous crime; because it is viewed by me not as a mere single grain
> of sand, but as a grain of sand added to an already accumulated moun-
> tain.

And again:

> I find that an exceedingly close walk with God is necessary for the
> maintaining of fervour in intercession. Sometimes an extraordinary
> sense of want may beget fervour in our petitions, or a peculiar mercy
> enliven our grateful acknowledgements; but it is scarcely ever that
> we can *intercede* with fervour unless we enjoy our habitual near-
> ness to God.

The heavenly intercourse of which the path on the roof was the silent witness was but the maturity of the spirit which had been given him from the first. Thomason, as far back as 1794, writes of a day when Marsden, afterwards of New Zealand, then an intimate young friend of Simeon's, entering Simeon's rooms, found him 'so absorbed in the contemplation of the Son of God, and so overpowered with a display of His mercy to his soul, that he was incapable of pronouncing a single word', till at length, after an interval, in a tone of strange significance, he exclaimed 'Glory, glory'. And then, a few days later, Thomason himself found him, at the hour of the private lecture on Sunday evening, scarcely able to discourse, 'from a deep humiliation and contrition'. If I have depicted Simeon's life at all aright, the alternating excesses of an ill-balanced mind; they were the two poles of a sphere of profound experience; the utterances of the heart of a true man, who was the servant of daily duty, but who really 'heard the words of God and saw the vision of the Almighty'.

But now from the roof we descend to the rooms, and to the large private meetings held there week by week for many years during term-time. These shall be described in the words of two eye-witnesses. The first account, preserved by Mr. Carus, is given in a letter written to 'Charlotte Elizabeth':

I must bring you into Mr. Simeon's audience-chamber, where my mind's eye sees him seated on a high chair at the right hand side of the fire-place. Before him are the benches, arranged for the occasion, occupied by his visitors. Even the window-recesses are furnished with seats, which, however, are usually filled the last, notwithstanding the repeated assurances of our venerated friend, somewhat humorously expressed, that he has taken special pains to make the windows air-tight, and has even put the artist's skill to the test

with a lighted candle. 'I shall be very glad,' he would say, 'to catch
from you every cold that you catch from the draught of my windows.' At the entry of each gownsman he would advance towards
the opening door, with all that suavity and politeness which you know
he possessed in a remarkable degree, and would cordially tender
his hand; and I assure you we deemed it no small honour to have had
a hearty shake of the hand and a kind expression of the looks from
that good old man.

As soon as the ceremony of introduction was concluded, Mr.
Simeon would take possession of his accustomed elevated seat and
would commence the business of the evening. I see him even now,
with his hands folded upon his knees, his head turned a little to one
side, his visage solemn and composed, and his whole deportment
such as to command attention and respect. After a pause, he would
encourage us to propose our doubts, addressing us in slow, and soft,
and measured accents:- 'Now – if you have any question to ask – I
shall be happy to hear it – and to give what assistance I can.' Presently one and then another would venture with his interrogatories,
each being emboldened by the preceding inquirer, till our backward-
ness and reserve were entirely removed. In the meantime two wait-
ers would be handing the tea to the company; a part of the entertainment which the most of us could well have dispensed with, as it
somewhat interrupted the evening's proceedings; but it was most
kindly provided by our dear friend who was always very considerate
of our comfort and ease.

It is my purpose, if you will so far indulge me, to give the substance of some conversations which took place in Mr. Simeon's
rooms, on May 3, 1833. This was the most interesting and solemn
Friday evening meeting that I ever attended. I never saw the holy
man of God more full of the spirit of his Master. His words were
distilled as honey from his lips; at least they were very sweet to *my*
taste; and their savour, I trust, I have still retained. On that memorable evening such a deep sense of his own unworthiness rested upon
his soul that he was low in self-abasement before God. All his language seemed to be, 'Lord, I am vile'; and his very looks spake the
same.

While the impression was fresh and vivid upon my mind, I wrote
down his observations, on leaving the room, as correctly as my

memory would allow. In order to be concise, I shall give them as proceeding directly from his mouth, together with the questions with which they originated. By this plan you will be able to see in what way these meetings were conducted.

When he suspected that any of his hearers were desirous to draw him upon controverted ground, he would soon put an end to their design by a short and pithy reply. Of this the following is an instance, which occurred on the same evening: 'What does the Apostle mean, sir, when he says, in 1 Timothy 4:10, that God is the Saviour of all men, specially of those that believe?'

Mr. Simeon replied: 'Of all, potentially; of them that believe, effectually. Does that make it clear to you?' Then, to render the subject practical, he added, 'Faith is a simple apprehension of Christ. It is not merely believing that He is the Saviour of the world, but it is believing in Him as peculiarly suited to our own individual cases. It is not the saying, Oh, now I see I am to be saved in this way, or in that way; this, so far as it goes, is very well; but the Gospel simply declares, "Believe on the Lord Jesus Christ, and thou shalt be saved".'

'What is the way to maintain a close walk with God?'

'By constantly meditating on the goodness of God and on our great deliverance from that punishment which our sins have deserved, we are brought to feel our vileness and utter unworthiness; and while we continue in this spirit of self-degradation, everything else will go on easily. We shall find ourselves advancing in our course; we shall feel the presence of God; we shall experience His love; we shall live in the enjoyment of His favour and in the hope of His glory. Meditation is the grand means of our growth in grace; without it, prayer itself is an empty service. You often feel that your prayers scarcely reach the ceiling; but oh, get into this humble spirit by considering how good the Lord is, and how evil you all are, and then prayer will mount on wings of faith to heaven. The sigh, the groan of a broken heart, will soon go through the ceiling up to heaven, aye, into the very bosom of God.'

The second picture is drawn by Canon Abner Brown:

It was wont to be said that the natural hastiness of Mr. Simeon's temper showed itself in irritable replies to the young men at the evening parties. The writer never himself observed anything of the kind, even when a silly question was asked, although he does remember to have once or twice heard a somewhat sharp rebuke given in answer to some flippant or rude question, such as it ill became any youth to ask of any honoured and grey-headed minister. And even when Simeon had passed over an unseemly question unreproved, the writer has occasionally heard undergraduates, after leaving the rooms, say to a companion, 'What a fool So and So must be to ask such a childish question!' or, 'It was a great deal too bad of So and So to bother and try to entrap old Simeon that way'; or, 'I wonder Simeon did not show him the door.'

Most who attended his parties, however, will remember the suite of marble tables, with gilded but very slender legs, which stood against his drawing-room walls. For these he had a great value, because they had belonged to a deceased relative or friend; and being nervously watchful at *crowded* Friday evening parties lest any of the young men should unconsciously damage them, his fear of their being thrown down led him, a very few times during the writer's entire residence, to utter a too hasty caution when he saw any guest leaning against them; but the irritable tone was gone again in a moment ....

The meetings most generally known and attended were the Friday tea-parties. Mr. Simeon was accustomed, for a long course of years, to have every Friday what he called an open day, when all who chose went at six o'clock to take tea with him in his rooms, every one asking what questions he would, and receiving an answer longer or shorter as might be. Hence a great variety of subjects came under review, subjects which could not be discussed in the pulpit. There was neither exposition, as such, nor prayer, and the party lasted until the clock struck seven. The numbers varied with the state of the term, but not unfrequently sixty or eighty were present; seated on chairs and benches arranged for the occasion round the room, and occupying even the recesses of the windows. All were accustomed to arrive punctually and together, so as to avoid commotion in the room after Simeon had taken his seat and the two servants had begun to hand tea round. Cordially, and with the suavity and politeness for which he was remarkable, he would welcome each gownsman as announced; and if any stranger to him were introduced, would also

note down his name and college in his private pocket memoran-
dum-book. After the arrivals had ceased, Mr. Simeon's usual place
was on an unbacked chair by the right hand of the fireplace, in full
view of the amphitheatre of faces round him; his little old quarto
Bible within his reach, his hands either folded on his knees, or quietly rubbed against each other, a motion which in him seemed to
indicate an exuberance of placid gladness, just as a child's clapping
its hands is a mark of its glee. His eye full of cheerful affection, his
countenance slightly raised, so as not to seem fixed on any individual, he sought to please and encourage as well as instruct, and
quickly placed every one as much as possible at ease. He would
often make some lively and playful remark as the young men were
coming in, or when he saw any constraint among his youthful guests.
Thus, if the name announced were a common name, as Brown, Smith,
Jones, etc., he would say, 'Brown, Brown – no name at all, sir! Is it
Brown of Trinity, Brown of Queens, or who?' or would relate some
little anecdote with the same object. By degrees one or another
grew bold enough, even before such an assembly of his companions
(no slight ordeal), to ask the venerable man a question. The ques-
tioning part, however, was usually in the hands of a few, by a kind of
tacit understanding that the conversation should be as much as possible left to Simeon himself. One or two also were often spokes-
men for a number of their more nervous friends. It seldom (but it
would be incorrect to say *never*) occurred that any gownsman was
forward or ready to display his own talents rather than draw instruction from Mr. Simeon; in general, there was no unseemly conduct
of the kind. Occasionally some well-known minister who might be
visiting Cambridge and Simeon, and who had himself been of the
Friday parties when he was young, would be present, and take an
active share in the conversation. In every possible way did Simeon
endeavour to make these tea-parties both useful and agreeable, and
to prevent disappointment to those young friends who had, as he
loved to say, honoured him with their company.

One Friday Mr. Simeon was taken suddenly and seriously ill,
when it was too late in the day to make his illness known through
the various colleges; and yet he was unwilling to have his young
guests turned back from his door at six o'clock. While the men
were arriving, the servant privately showed three of those (the writer

being one) who had been most frequent in attending the parties, into
the sick-room, and Mr. Simeon persuaded us to go through the ordeal (no trifle), not only of telling our sixty or seventy assembled
brother undergraduates how the case stood, but also of starting, and
keeping up for the usual time, some suitable conversation, such as
was customary on other occasions. We did so, and our fellow-stu-
dents kindly and heartily lending us their aid, the hour was passed in
useful Scriptural conversation; the good-humoured critique which
we afterwards heard pronounced by our companions being only that
which, in those days, the gownsmen usually applied to what fell from
every other minister or expositor than himself, viz., that it was
'Simeon and water'.

Occasionally the whole of an ordinary Friday party was occupied in remarks and hints which more strictly belonged to sermon-
party subjects; for Simeon knew that the majority of the men who
attended the larger never attended the smaller class of parties; and
he often therefore spoke in the larger or tea-party on points important for all who might possibly thereafter enter into Holy Orders,
even if they did not wish to attend the sermon-parties.

Another class of conversation-parties were the small occasional
gatherings at Mr. Simeon's own rooms, or at the houses of his intimate friends, ladies in both cases being frequently present. Sometimes it was a small dinner-party, sometimes an evening tea-party
after Hall; and these were held more frequently in vacation time, or
when some eminent minister, missionary, or layman, with whom he
happened to be intimate, was in Cambridge. The conversation was
of course for a time general, and usually on subjects interesting to
the Christian community at large; but after tea was over, it remained
in the hands of Simeon and one or two of the senior guests, and the
evening was closed after the manner of family prayers by one of
Simeon's wonderfully rich and beautiful expositions of some Scripture passage, the chief points of which he condensed into a short
concluding prayer at parting. Although such meetings were only
social gatherings of friendly hospitality, yet the discussions at them
bore strongly on the various important movements in progress
through the Christian world. In connection with one of these friendly
meetings, the writer remembers an incident highly characteristic
of the good old man's playful kindness. He had received for himself

and his wife an invitation from Mr. Simeon to an evening party, which, however, he was compelled to decline from having engaged to his own house for the same evening a small party of clergymen and married gownsmen. But Mr. Simeon would take no denial, and, without inquiring who the invited might be, insisted that the writer should tell every one of his expected guests, ladies and gentlemen alike, that his drawing-room for that evening 'was in Mr. Simeon's rooms at King's College', and should bring them all, without exception, to his evening party; which arrangement was accordingly carried out, to the great enjoyment and advantage of the writer's guests.

Brown's *Recollections* afford large materials for an estimate of the character and value of the Friday evenings. Allowing for some inevitable defects, they were on the whole a school of manly Christian thought and of practical good sense in dealing with problems of the Christian life. A few specimen paragraphs may be given.

Christian Liberty – This must not be used as a cloak for licentiousness; and yet we are all too fond of a Judaizing spirit, such as 'Touch not, taste not, handle not'. We ought to seek a tender conscience, but not a scrupulous one, nor a superstitious one.

There is a rule that will carry us safely through any difficulty in the way of compliance with the world as to matters which are right or wrong, not *per se*, but *par accident*. Where we give way on account of, or for the sake of pleasing others to their edification, or of doing good, we generally do right. We may not give way for the sake of *pleasing* any man, but only for the sake of *pleasing to edification*. No compliance is allowable in a thing wrong per se. Our first inquiry should be, Is the thing wrong *per se*? or only so in its accidental circumstances, being harmless in itself? Our spirit is so Judaizing that, if we dared, we would blame many things even in our Lord's life – for instance, His going to a marriage feast, His miracle in making wine ....

Persons say that Jesus never smiled. We do not read, at least, that He did; yet He gave thanks, rejoiced, wept, – had the feelings of a man. But I can never enter into any comparison between myself

and Christ. His high and holy office was infinitely above all others
in solemn importance; and His never smiling is no rule against our
smiling, because we are not in His circumstances ....

Christian liberty and legal bondage may be explained thus: The
Law requires everything and promises nothing. The Gospel gives
commandments and requires much, but promises to give everything
which it requires of us. The Gospel, therefore, is a delight and a
cause of gladness and rejoicing.

My brother disregarded deep religion, and said to me, 'You ask
too much.' I prayed much for him, and one day said, 'Is it too much
to love God with all your heart, and your neighbour as yourself?' He
said 'No'. 'Then,' said I, 'I will never ask more of you than this.' I
had thus his assent to a simple truth, which I could explain by Scripture, and this simple remark was made by God the means of my
brother's conversion. His full-length portrait hangs in my drawing-
room, and my rooms are full of memorials of him.

Confirmation – I think it was introduced as corresponding to the
sacred law which required all Jewish children of twelve years old to
go up and be presented in the Temple. Jesus did so, and may thus
seem to have recommended it to us. Confirmation is, however,
highly valuable as giving a minister contact with his flock; as opening their minds, at a peculiar season of life, and with the power of
specific duty, to instructions which else would come sleepily on
them. Nor does the abuse of it render its omission proper. Surely
the evil which meets the children at the avenues to the cathedral or
church may be much guarded against .... The new Bishop of London
(Dr. Blomfield) is about to make Confirmations annual and the parties of Catechumens small, which will cause the ordinance to be
much more what it was designed to be.

Christian Conversation – In conversation we are often more inclined to enter on the speculative rather than on the practical and
heart-searching topics of religion. If we had more holiness of heart,
it would not be so; but both classes of subject are good in their
place.

A variety of conversation is good. Students scruple at times about
studying their mathematics, because they say such study deadens

their spirituality. Let them see whether the fault is in them or in the studies; perhaps they are just as much deadened by any other subject. When the attention is constantly and closely directed to spiritual matters, during the intervals of study, or business, or earthly duty, perhaps more real progress is made than in those cases where spiritual subjects occupy the whole and the continual attention. A man and wife could not always confine their conversation to explicitly religious subjects, nor would it be proper. Wesley tells of a young woman, a domestic servant, who gave up her service that she might devote her time wholly to God; but she felt not the same peace, and life, and spirit in constant meditation, which she had felt in her daily duty. She returned to her proper calling, and God's presence returned to her again. We must look for God's blessing, and presence, and peace, in our lawful calling, and in the meditations allowed by the intervals of it.

Various minds are differently constituted, and all would not enjoy constant or deep religious talk; it should be varied, as in these our evening parties. With congenial minds, and when the circle is five or six, we can be deeply solemn, and enter, as it were, within the veil; but not so with all, nor with a circle of many persons. Flavel says, 'I can talk about religion with many, but there are few with whom I can talk religion itself.' I lately expressed my impression that one of the holiest men of our age was unfit for an important particular station, as to the filling up of which I was consulted, because he wanted elasticity of mind. He could not, I was sure, become all things to all men. It is a minister's duty to be so.

Metaphors – Do not give way to metaphor and figure, nor follow out Scripture figures too far. Brilliancy and imagery please us, but they draw our attention away from the truth contained in the text. A sober, solid, living divine (Dr. G.) was asked, it is said, his opinion of a richly splendid sermon of one of the most popular Cambridge preachers, and a really good man. His reply was, 'I could not attend to the sermon for the splendid imagery; it was incessantly flash, flash, flash, till it put my eyes out!' Now perhaps it may be my peculiarity of taste, but I always reject imagery when it occurs to my mind in preaching. I want to keep my people's attention off the preacher, off the manner, and to rivet it upon the truth which I have to tell. Other minds may have different ways of bringing out truth and producing effects; but I think you who are looking forward to the ministry will thank me hereafter for cautioning you strongly against the use of imagery and a flowery style. Get at the heart with the truth, not at the feelings by brilliancy.

Personal Reminiscences – For the first twenty-four years of my ministry I went on without a single Sabbath's intermission. I was then a whole year breaking down. For the next thirteen years I was quite lost to work, often unable to preach at all, seldom more than once a day, unfit for my weekly Tuesday parties with my parochial congregation. After a little more speaking than usual in those days, I was unable to walk across the room. I was often unable to speak, and was forced to point to what I wanted. My whole system used to collapse, as an infant's, and then I had hardly life in me. After this term it pleased God to restore me all at once, and for the last ten years I have been getting stronger.

I am not much afraid of true religion getting too fashionable, for I have been too long in the forefront of the battle, and I know the enmity of the human heart to it. But I do stand amazed at the marvellous change which is taking place all round in all ranks.

In the account of these evenings given by Canon Brown, it was noticed that no prayer was offered. As a fact, prayer was deliberately omitted by Simeon, lest he should come within the range of the stern Conventicle Act, and that he might keep his parties from even the suspicion of technical irregularity. I find him writing thus to that remarkable man, the Rev. R. W. Sibthorp, who was attempting a similar work at Oxford:

Days are materially altered in two respects; much good is in existence and in progress now, so that the same irregular exertions that were formerly necessary do not appear to be called for in the present day; and our ecclesiastical authorities are more on the alert now to repress anything which may be deemed irregular. I should be disposed therefore to carry my cup more even than I did in former days; not that I would relax my zeal in the least degree, but I would cut off occasion from those who might be glad to find occasion against me. On this account I would not do anything which might subject me to the Conventicle Act. My own habit is this: I have an open day, when all who choose it come to take their tea with me. Every one is at liberty to ask what questions he will, and I give to them the best answer I can. Hence a great variety of subjects come under review, subjects which we could not discuss in the pulpit; and the young men find it a very edifying season. We have neither exposition, as such, nor prayer; but I have opportunity of saying all that my heart can wish, without the formality of a set ordinance .... You need not expound; but if there be any passage of Scripture which you think of peculiar importance for their consideration, you may easily, without being a conjuror, contrive to have their attention turned to it; and you can easily recommend the young men to pray over it in secret.

In the second account mention is made of Simeon's quick temper. This was his weak point in the circle of Christian consistency, as it is with too many who otherwise follow the will of God in personal conduct. There was much fire in his nature, and with all his depth of insight into the ways and secrets of grace he does not seem, till near the close of his course, to have seen there all the resources which lie treasured for us in our Redeemer for an internal victory which crushes no element of true character, but brings harmony into the whole. But who shall judge Simeon lightly, or as a censor, in this matter? One thing is certain, that his occasional hasty words and looks were each time repented of tenderly before God, and as often as possible confessed before men, whether his coevals or his juniors, his friends or his servants. It is surely less memorable that he sometimes lost patience in small things (though Christianity is never better illustrated than when peace rules a naturally restless spirit amidst petty vexations) than that a man so bold, so vigorous, so much disposed by nature to rush into impetuous action, should have been kept by a divine power, diligently sought and humbly welcomed, true to a long straight line of endurance, unselfishness, and practical wisdom.

But it is quite right that the side of failure should not be forgotten. Mr. Carus gives an instance, not a little amusing on one side, described to him by a common friend:

> You know how particular he was about stirring the fire; and there was also another and greater infirmity of his, of speaking at times, as if he were very angry, about mere trifles. We were one day sitting at dinner at Mr. Hankinson's, when a servant behind him stirred the fire in a way so *unscientific* that Mr. S. turned round and hit the man a thump in the back, to stay his proceedings. When he was leaving me, on horseback, after the same visit, my servant had put the wrong bridle upon his horse. He was in a hurry to be gone, and his temper broke out so violently that I ventured to give him a little humorous castigation. His cloak-bag was to follow him by coach; so I feigned a letter in my servant's name, saying how high his character stood in the kitchen, but that they could not understand how a gentleman who preached and prayed so well should be in such passions about nothing, and wear no *bridle* upon his tongue. This I signed 'John Softly', and deposited it in his cloak-bag. The hoax so far succeeded that at first he scarcely discovered it; but it afterwards produced two characteristic notes. The first was addressed (April 12, 1804) to 'John Softly' by 'Charles Proud and Irritable'; 'I most cordially thank you, my dear friend, for your kind and seasonable reproof.' The second was to John's master, a letter of intense confession and humiliation: 'I hope, my dearest brother, that when you find your soul nigh to God, you will remember one who so greatly needs all the help he can get. *Naturam expellas furca, tamen usque recurret.* If I could but put *gratiâ* instead of *furcâ*, I would knock this adage on the head .... I open this again to entreat that, if John's mind was hurt by my conduct, you will tell him that I earnestly beg his pardon.'

Chapter 13

Closing Years

The story of the latter years of Simeon's life is bright and peaceful. We have already seen how much the troubled waters of his earlier days had subsided. His Gospel had not lost its offence, and to be called a Sim was never pleasant; but he was on the whole an object of great personal respect in the University and very widely influential in the Church. The late Lord Macaulay, son of his friend Zachary Macaulay, took his degree in 1822, and had ample opportunities for watching Simeon and his work. Looking back, in the year 1844, he writes to one of his sisters: 'As to Simeon, if you knew what his authority and influence were, and how they extended from Cambridge to the most remote corners of England, you would allow that his real sway over the Church was far greater than that of any Primate.'[1]

The life of the University was fast changing around him, in the direction of greater energy, a larger range of studies, and on the whole better order. It is interesting to recollect that his long evening was the morning or the noon of life for such Cambridge men as Sedgwick, Herschel, Peacock, Whewell, Julius Hare, William Mill, Thirlwall, Maurice, Trench, and Tennyson. In one of Brown's *Recollections* occurs a notice of Simeon's reasons for voting, at the election of a University member in 1829, for 'Cavendish', the Second Wrangler of that year.[2] In 1834 he speaks of the delight with

1. Life of Lord Macauley, I. 67, note.
2. This was William, Duke of Devonshire, who later became Chancellor of the University.

which he had read more than once Whewell's Bridgewater
Treatise. His own interests were fixed and concentrated im-
movably upon his spiritual ministry; but he both cordially
respected the scholars and learned men around him, and was
respected by them. Professor Sedgwick held him in charac-
teristically ardent regard.[3] He once stopped the old man in
the street, to exclaim with generous warmth on the contrast
between his own earthward geological labours and Simeon's fruitful work for heaven. I possess a letter of Sedgwick's,
written to me in 1869, in which he recalls conversations with
Simeon, and particularly his mentions of Martyn: 'I have many
times, in private society, heard Mr. Simeon, of King's, speak
with a kind of rapture of his beloved son, Henry Martyn, and
never without a faltering voice and a moist eye.' When
Simeon died, Sedgwick speaks of him with reverence in one
of his delightful letters,[4] adding the little incident – a quaint
tribute to a great memory – that when about that time three
lions were brought in a show to the town, the undergraduates
dubbed them Whewell, Sedgwick, and Simeon.

The record of those years of green old age is to be gathered chiefly from the letters and scraps of diary (Simeon
never persevered long in diary-keeping) preserved in Canon
Carus' Memoir. Here and there occur allusions to public
events, as he watched them from his busy retreat. Thus he
writes to Thomason, December 24th, 1817:

> The papers will tell you all about the death of the Princess Char-
> lotte of Wales. She died in child-bed. The whole nation was ready to
> rejoice at the birth of an heir to the throne; but it pleased God to
> take away both the mother and child, and the whole land was thrown

3. See Life and Letters of Sedgwick, ii. 122, for a warm eulogy of Simeon, written
after a perusal of Carus's Memoir.
4. Life and Letters, I. 468.

into consternation. I suppose that no event ever penetrated the nation with such grief. At Cambridge the pulpit at St. Mary's and the reading-desk and throne were all put into mourning; and the day of her funeral was spontaneously kept throughout the land as a Sabbath. At St. Mary's, the Regius Professor of Divinity, Dr. Kaye, preached to a congregation not seated but jammed. We assembled in the Senate-house yard to St. Mary's. Every pulpit in the town too is in mourning. Nothing but black is seen anywhere.

Poor Prince Leopold will feel himself a stranger now in this land, and will doubtless go back again to his own country. He has behaved nobly on the occasion, and gained the hearts of the whole country. Were he to die now, there would be nothing but busts and monuments all the kingdom over. In a year's time his name will scarcely be known.

He could not foresee the long future of the adviser of Europe. In 1820, to the same friend, he alludes to the Cato Street Conspiracy: 'P.S. – I never touch on news or politics, but the nation is in a dreadful state. You will have heard of the conspiracy to destroy all the King's ministers.'

In 1822 he touches in his diary on the subject of 'Catholic Emancipation', and the circumstances are interesting, as they bring him and his friend Charles Grant, the East India Director, into one scene on opposite sides:

November 19. Old Mr. Grant, with Professor Farish, called on me and dined with me. It was a great grief to me that I could not vote for his son on Tuesday next; but I told him that I regard my vote, not as a right, but as a trust, to be used conscientiously for the good of the whole kingdom; and his son's being a friend to what is called Catholic Emancipation is in my eyes an insurmountable objection to his appointment. Gladly would I give to Catholics every privilege that could conduce to their happiness; but to endanger the Protestant ascendancy and stability is a sacrifice which I am not prepared to make. Viewing this matter as I do, I could not vote for Mr. Robert Grant, if he were my own son.

In 1822 he had visited Ireland, with his dear friend William Marsh, to promote their dearest common interest, the Jewish missions. He was now sixty-three; and he writes to Thomason: 'Now for Ireland. You will wish to hear of my motions in my climacteric, more especially as my dial has been "put back ten degrees".' And then follows a lively record of his Irish enterprise, which was begun and ended within eight days altogether. 'No sooner were we arrived, than Irish hospitality evinced itself in an extraordinary degree. You, who know the precise line in which I walk at Cambridge, will be astonished, as I myself was, to find Earls and Viscounts, Deans and Dignitaries, calling upon me, and Bishops desirous to see me.'

On his way home he stayed a few days at Oxford, which he had visited first in far-off 1783, when he preached to a large congregation at Carfax. He now saw Copleston, Provost of Oriel, afterwards Bishop of Llandaff, 'with whom I dined, and held most profitable conversation. He accords more with my views of Scripture than almost any other person I am acquainted with.'

In 1823 he paid the visit to Paris of which I have spoken above, when he was introduced to the Duchesse de Broglie. In that year he preached at St. Mary's on 'The Law and the Gospel'; as courageously, yet as carefully, as ever. However, the sermons displeased some of the then University officials, and for seven years he did not get another invitation to the pulpit. But at this very time he records with joy the great change for the better in the University, in respect of religion: 'The sun and moon are scarcely more different from each other than Cambridge is from what it was when I was first minister of Trinity Church; and the same change has taken place in the whole land.'

A memorandum of 1826 is interesting:

Last week three Bishops did me the honour of visiting me: Dr. Burgess, Bishop of Salisbury, Dr. Law, Bishop of Bath and Wells, Dr. Jebb, Bishop of Limerick; and I accompanied them to King's Chapel and to Trinity Library, and spent above an hour with them. This shows how much Christian liberality has increased and is increasing. I am not conscious that I am one atom less faithful to my God than in former days, or more desirous of human favour; yet God is pleased thus graciously to honour me. In former years I should as soon have expected a visit from three crowned heads as from three persons wearing a mitre; not because there was any want of condescension in them, but because my religious character affixed a stigma to my name. I thank God that I receive this honour as from Him, and am pleased with it no further than as it indicates an increasing regard for religion among my superiors in the Church, and may tend to lessen prejudice among those to whom the report of it may come.

To 1827 belongs, I think, an incident preserved by Brown: William Ellis, missionary in the South Seas, told it at a meeting at Cambridge, in October, 1829. He said that as he left Hawaii, or as it was then written, Owhyhee, for home, a native magnate who had lately visited England charged him to carry his earnest greetings to the Bishop of Portsmouth. He was assured that such a dignitary did not exist; but he was certain of the man, and described his venerable appearance, and the occasion on which he had seen him. Just before he and other Hawaians had sailed from Portsmouth, leaving their King and Queen (victims of small-pox) in an English grave, the Bishop had come on board to sympathise with their sorrow, and had spoken solemnly of the Christian's God, and entreated them to seek Him, and then had prayed with them and given them his blessing. Ellis had found, through the ship's captain, that the mysterious Bishop was no other than Simeon.

In 1829, he kept the jubilee of his unbroken Cambridge

residence, and asked a few of his nearest friends to spend
two days with him, 'in social and religious exercises'. The
Diary records those days:

> The first evening was very sweet. I opened my views of a jubilee
> (like the prodigal, whose joy would be not only tempered by, but
> almost wholly consist in, a retrospective shame and prospective de-
> termination through grace to avoid in future the evils from which
> God's free mercy, founded on the Atonement, has delivered us). *It
> was proclaimed on the day of Atonement* (see Leviticus 25:9).
> The second day we met at eleven o'clock. I read some portions of
> Scripture and prayed for the divine presence. Then Mr. Sargent read,
> and gave a prayer of humiliation; then Mr. Daniel Wilson followed
> for the Universities; then Dr. Steinkopf for the religious Societies
> and for the Church. We then separated for an hour. Mr. Hawtrey
> ended with thanksgiving. Mr. D. Wilson preached the Lecture (at
> Trinity Church) .... Blessed be God for this mercy.'

William Wilberforce had been invited, but was too weak
to come. He wrote a letter full of love and sympathy, and
closed with a brief comment on the past:

> The degree in which, without any sacrifice of principle, you have
> been enabled to live down the prejudices of many of our higher
> ecclesiastical authorities, is certainly a phenomenon I never ex-
> pected to witness.

About the time of this bright jubilee two heavy bereave-
ments befell him. Thomason died, and then another beloved
friend, a brother-Fellow, Thomas Lloyd. Simeon says of
Lloyd: 'A more perfect character I knew not upon earth. He
was pre-eminently dear to me, as being my own son in the
faith, the very firstfruits of Achaia. He is gone a little before
us.' And then he thinks of his own work and his own approaching rest: 'Through mercy I possess at present very pe-

culiar vigour both of body and mind; both of which I need for the completing of my Appendix of six volumes, or 700 discourses, now in the press. I print and revise a volume of about 600 close pages every month. Three volumes are now finished, and, I hope, to be out in October; after which time I have a kind of presentiment, which I delight to indulge, that I shall speedily be called home. But I am willing to wait, and delighted to work while it is day. Never was my work more delightful to me than at the present moment. But I seem to be so near the goal that I cannot but run with all my might .... Soon, very soon shall we meet our beloved brother again, and join with him in everlasting hallelujahs to God and to the Lamb.'

But a long sunset hour of work lay still before him. In 1831 he preached for the last time before the University, with no abatement of spiritual, mental, or bodily force. His theme was the revealed Work of the Holy Spirit; the running text of the sermons was Romans 8:9: 'If any man have not the Spirit of Christ, he is none of His.' Daniel Wilson, Bishop of Calcutta, recalled those occasions in a paper of recollections written in India after Simeon's death:

The vast edifice was literally crowded in every part. The Heads of Houses, the Doctors, the Masters of Arts, the Bachelors, the Undergraduates, the congregation from the town, seemed to vie with each other in eagerness to hear the aged and venerable man. His figure is now before me. His fixed countenance, his bold and yet respectful manner of address, his admirable delivery of a well-prepared discourse, his pointed appeal to the different classes of his auditory, the mute attention with which they hung upon his lips, all composed the most solemn scene I ever witnessed.

Here let me quote a reminiscence of Simeon, as he was seen in private at this time by his friends. It is written by that great Christian, Joseph John Gurney, of Earlham Hall, Simeon's friend, brother of the philanthropic saint, Elizabeth Fry, and of Hannah, Lady Buxton:

Memoranda of an afternoon spent at Cambridge, April, 1831.
After ordering dinner, we sallied forth for a walk; but first sent a note to our dear friend, Charles Simeon, to propose spending part of the evening with him. While we were absent from the inn, there arrived a small characteristic note, hastily written by him in pencil, – 'Yes, yes, yes, – Come immediately and dine with me.' Simeon has the warm and eager manners of a foreigner with an English heart beneath them. He is full of love towards all who love his Master, and a faithful sympathising friend to those who have the privilege of sharing in his more intimate affections. To all around him, whether religious or worldly, he is kind and courteous; and by this means, as well as by the weight of his character, he has gradually won a popularity at Cambridge which now seems to triumph over all prejudice and persecution. He is upwards of seventy years of age, but his eye is not dim, his joints not stiffened, his intellect not obscured. His mind, lips, eyes, and hands move along together in unison. And singularly pliable and rapid is he both in his mental and bodily movements, quick to utter what he feels, and to act what he utters. His conversation abounds in illustrations, and while all his thoughts and words run in the channel of religion, he clothes them with brightness and entertainment, and men, women, and even children are constrained to listen. It is not, however, the ear alone which he engages; while his conversation penetrates that organ even when uttered in its lowest key (so distinct are his whispers), the eye is fixed on his countenance, which presents an object of vision peculiarly grotesque and versatile, and at the same time affecting. Nor are his hands unwatched by the observer, while they beat time to the very-varying emotions of his mind.

Simeon. 'I preach to the people with my tongue, my eyes, and my hands; and the people receive what I say with their ears, their eyes, and their mouths.'

We declined his invitation to dinner, and had no intention of intruding upon him before the evening; but as we were walking near

King's College, we heard a loud halloo behind us, and presently saw
our aged friend, forgetful of the gout, dancing over the lawn to meet
us. Although the said lawn is forbidden ground, except to the Fellows of the College, we could not do otherwise than transgress the
law on such an occasion; and our hands were soon clasped in his
with all the warmth of mutual friendship. He then became our guide
and led us through several of the colleges.

We reached the new Hall of King's, just as the dinner was await-
ing him. 'You see I have taken leave of the gout,' said he merrily, as
he leaped up the steps ...

As we were enjoying our cup of tea, our dear friend continued to
converse in his own peculiar manner. We were speaking of the importance of universal kindness:

Simeon. 'I am sorry when I hear a religious person say, The world
insults me, therefore I will insult the world. They speak evil of me,
and deride me, and mock me; it is with better reason that I do the
same towards them. My dear brother, I should say to such a man,
You are quite in error .... When the early disciples were persecuted,
it was to turn to a testimony for them. So it will be with you: the
world will mock and trample on you; a man shall come and, as it
were, slap you on the face. You rub your face, and say, This is strange
work; I like it not, Sir. Never mind; I say, "This is your evidence; it
turns to you for a testimony.'

We spoke of his having gradually surmounted persecution, and
of his being now so popular, that nearly 120 Freshmen were lately
introduced to him. He ascribed the abatement of prejudice to his
twenty volumes of Sermons, in which no one could find anything
heretical. I attributed it (I believe with greater justice) to his kindness and courtesy, and to the force of truth.

When we reverted to the subject of suffering for Christ's sake,
he said, 'My dear brother, we must not mind a little suffering. When
I am getting through a hedge, if my head and shoulders are safely
through, I can bear the pricking of my legs. Let us rejoice in the
remembrance that our holy Head has surmounted all His sufferings
and triumphed over death. Let us follow Him patiently; we shall
soon be partakers of His victory.'

Simeon. 'I could say to a Christian friend, I can tell you what is
perfect religion. Can you indeed? Surely it can be no easy matter to

define it. I will do it, my brother, in a few simple words: perfect religion is to the soul what the soul is to the body. The soul animates the whole person; it sees through the eye, hears through the ear, tastes through the mouth, handles through the hands, talks through the tongue, reflects through the brain. The whole body is moved and regulated by an impulse from within. Let religion take full possession of the soul, and it will be found to actuate all its movements and direct all its powers. There will be no violent efforts, no stiffness, no awkwardness. All will be natural and easy; and unseen and gentle influence will pervade the whole mind and regulate the whole conduct; and the creature will gradually become conformed to the image of his Creator. This, my brother, is perfect religion.'

We had afterwards some interesting conversation on the right method to be aimed at in the exercise of the Christian Ministry. Although he and I have been accustomed to different views in relation to this subject, I was glad to listen to him, and felt that there was much in the hints he gave me which it would be well for Friends as well as others to observe.

Simeon. 'When I compose a sermon, I take a single text, and consider the main subject to which it relates as the warp. The peculiar language in which it is couched supplies me with the woof. The series of cross-threads with which I weave the subject may be handled in various ways. You may take it up by the right-hand corner, or by the left-hand corner, or by a projection in the middle.' (While he said this he was handling a little parcel on the table by way of illustration.) 'But you must never wander beyond its true limits, you must not patch up your text by borrowing any extraneous ideas from other passages of Scripture. The ancients used to say, There is a man in every stone. Choose your stone, chisel away its outer covering, and keep to the man which you find in it. Canova would have regarded it as a disgrace to his profession had he patched into a statue even a little finger from a second block! Ministers differ very much from one another in their administration of religion. Some are for ever playing tenor, lifting up their hands with exultation, jingling their shrill bells. Others play nothing but bass, always grumbling and growling. Don't you hear that Eolian harp, my brother, its strings swept by the breeze, its melody gentle yet strong, varied yet harmonious? That is what the Christian Ministry ought to be – the genuine impartial Scripture played upon and applied under a divine influence – under the breath of heaven.'

The hour of the evening was advancing, and these beautiful remarks formed a happy conclusion to familiar conversation. His elderly servants were now called in, and I was requested to read the Scriptures .... A very precious solemnity ensued, during which the language of prayer and praise arose, I humbly hope, with acceptance. I believe that both my dear wife and myself were ready to acknowledge that we had seldom felt with any one more of 'the unity of the Spirit in the bond of peace'.

Gurney gives some 'additional memoranda':

I remember asking him one day, what he thought of that anxiety and depression of mind with respect to religion to which sincere Christians are often liable, an experience of which he did not himself appear to be much of a partaker. As far as I can recollect his reply, it was to the following effect: 'When such a state is excessive, there is probably physical disease, or there may be some secret fault, or some difficult duty still unperformed, disturbing the conscience, which then acts upon us as a tormentor; or there may be a mixing up of our own works with the plan, and only a partial and inadequate reliance upon Christ ...'

Yet this experienced Christian well knew what it was to mourn and be in bitterness. It was one of his grand principles of action, to endeavour at all times to honour his Master by maintaining a cheerful happy demeanour in the presence of his friends. No man could compare him to the spies who brought an evil report from the land of promise, and spoke only of the giants who dwelt in it. Rather was he like one coming forth from Canaan well laden with grapes for his own refreshment and for that of all his brethren. It was on the principle now mentioned, that he was accustomed to exercise at his own house a cheerful, liberal, and sometimes almost splendid hospitality. He considered that for such liberality a warrant might be found in the conduct of our blessed Lord Himself, who turned the water at the marriage feast into the very best wine, and who was accustomed to bless and sanctify by His presence the bounties of many a hospitable board. But the same Jesus set us an example of retirement into the desert for fasting and humiliation before God His Father. Thus also as a humble follower of the Saviour, Simeon in his private hours, as I have strong reasons for believing, was peculiarly broken and prostrate before the Lord. It was I am sure with undissembled feelings of humility that he sometimes spoke of his own salvation as of that which would be the very masterpiece of divine grace, and of the probability of his being the last and least in the kingdom of heaven ....

Though often so hoarse as to be scarcely capable of uttering anything but whispers, he was the best master of elocution I ever met with; and most obliging were his attempts to teach my guests, my children, and myself, how to manage the voice in reading and speaking. He used to advise us to address some near object in a whisper, then to speak by degrees more and more loudly, as the object was imagined to recede – afterwards to reverse the process, until we came back to a whisper. His rule was, that when a person begins and ends such an exercise in a natural whisper, it affords an evidence that the voice has been kept throughout in the right key. He strongly objected to all unnecessary heightening of the voice, or exertion of the lungs, commanding us with paternal authority not to expend a shilling on that which we could procure for a farthing! He considered that a little pains bestowed in this way on his brethren in the ministry was of no trifling consequence, even to the cause of religion: and on this ground, polite and tender as he was, and full of the most loving apologies to those whom he was instructing, he did not hesitate to mimic his friends in order to effect their cure. 'How did I speak this evening?' said a clerical friend to him, shortly after leaving his pulpit. 'Why, my dear brother,' said he, 'I am sure you will pardon me – you know it is all love, my brother – but indeed it was just as if you were knocking on a warming-pan – tin, tin, tin, tin, without any intermission!'

In 1832 fell the fiftieth anniversary of his appointment to be Minister of Trinity Church. The parishioners showed the heartiest regard for their once rejected pastor. 'October 1. At 11 o'clock five gentlemen came to present me with a valuable epergne; their address was most kind .... Such a testi-

mony of love from my hearers quite overcame me. I returned
them thanks as God enabled me, and with a prayer of thanksgiving I closed the interview.' At one o'clock he gave a dinner to 250 of his poor in the school-room in Trinity Place,
King Street. 'The room was decorated with boughs and flow-
ers. I implored a blessing on the food, and on the company
assembled. Mr. Carus sat at the head of the table on my right,
Mr. Hose on my left. All the heads of the parish sat at intervals to carve the dinner. Before it was over, I went round the
middle table, expressing love to those on either side. Then
the heads of the parish brought me a salver ... with something
of a set speech. I returned thanks with tears of gratitude and
love .... I am now come home somewhat fatigued, that I may
be still and quiet before the Evening Service.'

At that service he preached from 2 Peter 1:12-15, where
the aged Apostle 'puts his disciples in remembrance', before he lays aside 'this tabernacle', that 'after his decease'
they may remember. The church was thronged. The sermon
was printed immediately, and given to each parishioner, as *A
Pastoral Admonition to an affectionate Flock*. The next three
days he spent, like the other jubilee days of 1829, in his rooms
with his clerical friends, confessing, praying, and giving
thanks. Sargent, Bickersteth, Hankinson, Marsh, Close, were
of the company; Wilberforce again sent a glowing message
of affection.

Simeon writes to his old schoolfellow, Mitchell (now the
third survivor of the boyish circle, with Goodall, Provost of
Eton, and himself):

Who would ever have thought I should behold such a day as this?
My parish sweetly harmonious; my whole works stereo-typing in
twenty-one volumes, and my ministry not altogether inefficient at
the age of seventy-three .... But I love the valley of humiliation. I

there feel that I am in my proper place. There you also delight to walk; and our meeting on the heavenly hills will be, I trust, most blessed to us both.

The next year saw the end of his long labour over the publication of his works. Often before 1833 he had printed considerable sets of Sermons and Outlines; but now all these were collected, revised, and arranged. The last five volumes of the complete series of twenty-one reached him May 24, 1833. Archbishop Howley had accepted the dedication; and in June, Simeon was received in private audience by William the Fourth, and presented the books to the King. Marsh wrote him this short letter on the occasion:

'Seest thou a man diligent in his business? He shall stand before kings' (Prov. 22:29); *e.g. Mr. Simeon at Court.* So the *Courier* informs me, and I believe it, and therefore thank God. You have never preached on this text; and now you will be afraid to do it. Not because you have not experienced its truth, but because you have.

Copies were accepted by the Ambassadors, to be placed in the foreign libraries. It is curious, as a collocation of opposites, to read that Talleyrand duly received a set of Simeon's *Works* for France, and sent it to Paris.

He was asked again this year to preach before the University; the Vice-Chancellor called personally to make the proposal. But the gout had pulled him down, and he declined. Once more, as we shall see, he was to be asked, and to accept; but then death interrupted the fulfilment.

The enlargement of Trinity Church was a great interest of 1833 and 1834.

All through these closing years the indefatigable correspondence was continued, on very various subjects; on the problem of caste, stated to him by Bishop Wilson of Calcutta; on questions of the soul, raised by many friends. His own beloved themes, humiliation, contrition, adoration, appear more frequently than ever in his letters. He writes to Miss Mary Sophia Elliott, Henry Venn's granddaughter, and sister of the writer of the hymn, *Just as I am*: 'I would have the whole of my experience one continued sense – 1st, of my nothingness, and dependence on God; 2nd, of my guiltiness and desert before Him; 3rd, of my obligations to redeeming love, as utterly overwhelming me with its incomprehensible extent and grandeur. Now I do not see why any one of these should swallow up another. That they are separable in imagination, like the rays of light, I well know: but that they should be combined in action, I am well convinced.' And again, to her sister Eleanor: 'While thinking of you in my carriage today, a view of this subject occurred to my mind ... that this very humiliation will give to our happiness in heaven a tone that will elevate us above the highest archangels. The angels can sing in the *air*, but cannot from their own experience send forth the deep notes which will soften, and enlarge, and complete *our* songs.'

Chapter 14

The Last Months

I bring the reader to the year 1836. Simeon's health had been broken occasionally by severe attacks of gout. In 1834, in February, he had been so ill that his death was reported in Cambridge. He writes to Daniel Wilson, who had gone out to Calcutta in 1832, that the illness had been a time, as to the soul, not indeed of joyful emotions but of the peace of God. 'In God, and in God alone, I have all that I can need; and therefore my eyes are turned to Him always, Him exclusively, Him without the shadow of a doubt. Were I to look at Him through the medium of my own experience, it would be like looking at the sun through the medium of the waters; the sun would appear to move as the water undulates; whereas when viewed in Himself alone, He is uniformly and steadily the same, without any variableness or shadow of turning.'

The same deep rest in God breathes itself into another letter about this time to the same friend:

That you want a Grant and an Udny I greatly regret; but their God you have, and more you cannot have. In truth, I love to see the creature annihilated in the apprehension, and swallowed up in God; I am then safe, happy, triumphant. And I recommend to you to enter into the chambers of all His glorious perfections, and to shut the doors about you, and there abide till He shall have accomplished all the good purposes of His goodness both in you and by you. Nothing less than a mutual indwelling of God in us and of us in God will suffice – beyond that, we want nothing.

But he recovered considerably. Late in 1835 he writes

again to Wilson that he has 'been working double tides at Cambridge for seven weeks, and at Brighton (in Mrs. Elliott's house) one. Through mercy I am, for ministerial service, stronger than I have been at any time this thirty years ... preaching at seventy-six with all the exuberance of youth ... but looking for my dismission daily.'

The letters are as many and as interesting as ever. One beautiful answer of loving casuistry, to his friend Mary Elliott, is a true complement to the words just quoted in which he tells Wilson of Calcutta of his profound peace in God:

> In your letter of this morning you express a fear that you may love your dear Mother or a friend too much; and I am anxious to correct that idea without loss of time; first, because it is a source of disquiet to the conscience, and next because it is an error which almost universally prevails in the Church of God. That we may show our love improperly I readily grant; but that we can love one another too much I utterly deny, provided only it be in subserviency to the love of God. I think I have explained to you that word *fervently* ('see that ye love one another with a pure heart'): its precise meaning is *intensely*. No two words in any two languages more exactly agree than 'intensely' does with the original. If then our love be with a pure heart, this alone were sufficient to establish the point ....
>
> Christianity does not encourage apathy; it is to regulate, not to eradicate, our affections. It admits of their full operation, but tempers them as to their measure and sanctifies them to the Lord. I have often been comforted by knowing that Lazarus and his sisters were peculiarly loved of their Lord, and that John was an object of His more than ordinary attachment; and from hence you will see that, if I have written this for your instruction, I have had any eye also to my own vindication, if I should appear to err in the discharge of the most delightful of all duties.
>
> But I will not delay this, that I may show at least that, if love be a crime, there are few more guilty than your Friend,
>
> C. Simeon.

Earlier in the year he had described himself as 'only a poor pensioner soldier, wearing the King's uniform, and just twice a week attending the parade and discharging the domestic exercise that has been assigned'. Yet soon after writing so, he undertook and carried out a visitation of some of the churches in the patronage of his Trust, a journey of five hundred miles; to Bath, Hereford, Cheltenham, Birmingham, Lichfield, Darlaston, and Darley Dale. On the way he heard from Cambridge that he was 'appointed to preach before the University in November'. Not often in the history of the Cambridge pulpit has the office of Select Preacher been committed to a man far advanced in his seventy-seventh year; an office which in those days, as no longer now, implied the delivery of a course of four sermons. But Simeon at once accepted the nomination; indeed he had expected it, and was already armed with the manuscripts completed for delivery. Mr. Carus, in a little volume *Simeon on Preaching*, published as lately as 1887, makes special mention of this early preparation:

> His power of rapid composition and masterly discussion of texts was exhibited in a remarkable manner at the close of 1835. One of the Proctors, a Fellow of his own College, requested to be permitted to nominate him as Select Preacher for November the next year. Mr. Simeon was much moved at this privilege proposed to him at his advanced age, but said he must decline the kind offer, as he did not expect to live so long. 'But supposing,' said his friend, 'that we have the happiness to retain you here amongst us a little longer, as we fondly hope, you will not then refuse us?' Upon this Mr. Simeon gave his consent, and said, 'I will *at once* begin to prepare the four sermons.' And so he did, for I went to him soon after, when he had already composed the first sermon, which he read over to me, and told me to come again the next day, and I should hear the second; and that also was ready when I called, and so again the third and

fourth, all within a week. And then the first sermon was improved and entirely re-written.'

The subject of the course was well fitted to be the last of his life: 'A shadow of things to come; but the body is of Christ' (Col. 2:17). I have in my keeping the four manuscripts, written out in full, in a firm hand, and dated by anticipation, November 6, 13, 20, 27, 1836. They contain a plain, strong statement of the prophetic import of the ceremonial of the Old Testament, on the lines of interpretation authorised by the Epistle to the Hebrews. All is carefully worked out and put in order, and a table of contents is written at the end of the first manuscript. It is moving and instructive to see how, at the very end of his course, he still rests where he had first refuge in his great need; at the atoning Sacrifice. One sentence in the second sermon is an almost verbal echo of those words of Bishop Thomas Wilson's which had carried the message of hope to his soul in 1779:

> The ritual of the Law was to give to the Jewish people, as by a shadow preceding and projected by the substance, some views of a Saviour, and of the way in which a repenting and believing sinner might be saved. The most ignorant Jew, if interrogated how he was to obtain mercy at God's hands, might without a moment's hesitation answer, 'By sacrifice to be sure, and by means of a victim dying in my stead.'

Early in August he returned to Cambridge. 'This day week,' he writes from Darley, July 29, 'I shall, I hope, every hour be getting nearer to my dear people and to my blessed home. I am almost counting the hours till I reach my sweet abode. But from the first day I set off to the present hour I have been as highly favoured as a mortal and sinful being can well be. My intercourse has been with the excellent of the earth, and every one of them striving to the utmost of their power to show me kindness for the Lord's sake. If you could have seen my *meetings* anywhere, and my *partings* at Hereford and Lichfield, you would have known a little what love is.'

In a letter to Archdeacon Hodson, August 8, he speaks of his ministrations in his church:

> Yesterday I preached to a church as full as it could hold, and partook of the Lord's Supper in concert with a larger number than has been convened together on such an occasion in any church in Cambridge since the place existed upon earth. Before I came to the living, I attended once at Trinity Church to hear on some occasion a very popular preacher; and, as I then never turned my back upon the Lord's Supper, I staid during the administration of it, and was myself one of *three*, who besides the parson and clerk formed the whole number of the communicants. So greatly has the Church of England been injured by myself and my associates.

The day after writing to Hodson, another correspondent claimed him, 'a person under deep mental distress'. His answer closes thus:

> I have no wish to know your name. It is sufficient for me that you are a fellow-sinner in distress. The Lord, even our Great High Priest, has your name written on His breastplate; and that is my consolation when I am constrained, through forgetfulness, to express my intercessions generally; when, if I were able to spread before my God the names and states of all for whom I have been desired to pray, I would gladly do it. I hope, with tender sympathy, to spread your case before Him; and I entreat the favour of you to remember at the throne of grace one, who, if he be not distressed like you, needs quite as much the prayers and intercessions of others in his behalf, even
>
> Your faithful servant,
> C. Simeon.

The last sermon in Trinity Church was preached on Sunday, September 18. The text was 2 Kings 10:16; the incident

of Jehu and Jehonadab. The manuscript notes, written in the
same firm hand as ever, give a full outline of the treatment of
the subject. Some sentences are significant in the light of the
occasion:

> It is not sufficient for any man to run well for a season only. We
> must endure to the end, if ever we would be saved. Whatever your
> attainments may be, and whatever you may have done or suffered in
> the service of your God, you must forget the things that are behind,
> till you have actually fulfilled your course and obtained the crown.

Here let us pause a little, to look as it were at this old
man, as once more he leaves the north porch of Trinity Church
and walks back to King's College. We observe his face, his
bearing, his dress. He holds his head erect, almost more than
erect; his aquiline nose and prominent chin are full of character; his whole aspect seems to say cheerfully, *nitor in
adversum*. His stature is middle, but his upright pose makes
him look almost tall as he steps out quickly homeward. He
wears knee-breeches and cloth gaiters, the statutable dress
of every resident member of the University when he was
young, now in 1836 the garb only of old-fashioned old men;
and such his head-gear is also – a kind of short shovel hat.
His Master-of-Arts gown is large and full, and under his arm
we can see a bulky umbrella.

The old clergyman is no dignitary, nor has he ever dreamt
of dignities in the Church. But he has won a sure place among
the servants who enter into the joy of their Lord: and he has
gathered around him here, before as yet he passes in there, a
great moral authority and dignity. He has been the implement
in divine hands by which the highest blessings have been
brought directly to a multitude of hearts, and indirectly to
innumerable numbers, even in the most distant regions. As

regards the Church of England, his dearly beloved Mother Church, he has proved himself one of her truest servants and most effectual defenders. Perhaps more than any other one man who ever arose within her pale, he has been the means of showing, in word and in life, that those Christian truths which at once most abase and most gladden the soul, as it turns (in no conventional sense of the words) from darkness to light, from death to life, from self to Christ, are not the vagaries of a few fanatical minds, careless of order and of the past, but the message of the Church, the tradition of her noblest teachers, the breath and soul of her offices and order. He has shown, in another direction, under conditions of difficult experiment, that the converted life is, in its genuine development, a life of self-discipline, of considerateness for every one around, of courtesy and modesty, of hourly servitude to established duty, and of that daylight of truthfulness without which no piety can possibly be wholesome.

Shall I attempt an estimate of the exact relation between Simeon's work and that great movement towards a more positive ecclesiasticism which, already before he died, had set in within the Anglican borders? I will not venture upon detail; it would be interminable. But, speaking very briefly, I may say that from one side a line of sympathy may be traced between the two. So far as the movement which arose at Oxford was a reaction from an overdrawn individualism in religion and an excess of the subjective spirit, there was much in Simeon's thought and teaching which struck a concord with it. He loved ancient order and solemn ordinances, and he magnified the office of the Christian ministry. He greatly desired to see, not merely more energy in individual Christians, but more life and power in the English Church as such; he was, as we have seen, decidedly and thoughtfully a Churchman. The Evangelical revival of the eighteenth century found a certain defect supplied in the school of Simeon. Its earlier leaders, with really few exceptions, were by no means careless of the essential sacredness of order and cohesion; but they found themselves often in circumstances where at least there seemed to be 'a need of disorder'. Simeon, one with them in main spiritual principles, always in quest, like them, of individual conversions, was led both by his situation and his reflections to a more distinct sense than most of them had felt of the claims of corporate and of national religious life. And in this respect he would have found much to attract his interest and sympathies towards the Oxford movement in its earlier phases. There is another side, however, to consider. That movement drew much of its great strength from its assertion of truths forgotten, or imperfectly remembered, and which were the true complement of others made prominent by what had gone before. But I am not enough of an optimist to think that this was all; that the agitations of the past fifty years have been due to nothing but a revived assertion of a perfectly true ideal of the Christian Church and its work, and to hostility to that assertion. I hardly need say that in many important respects it was not continuity or development which led from the Evangelical to the Oxford revival, but a definite repudiation by the Tractarian leaders of some of the chief principles of the Evangelicals. The theory of the Church, the relation between the Church and the Scripture, and the doctrine of Justification, were handled by the Oxford writers not so as to develop and supplement the teaching of the other school, but so as to counteract it.

But I only thus state the case, and then avow my personal conviction that Simeon's conception of the scale and relations of the great Christian truths was to a remarkable degree faithful, not only to the Reformation theology, but to that of the New Testament. As that oldest of old fashions, change, persists, many things may come to be modified in religious usage, and even in the expression of religious thought. But I believe that no essential modification can be made in what was Simeon's characteristic message without a sorrowful loss to the Church, and to the Christian. He venerated order and authority. But he always also believed, and said, with living conviction, that the supreme religious necessity is that the individual should know God in Christ; that without the blood of the Atonement there is no remission; that without the effectual work of the heavenly Spirit there is no divine life and love in man; and that humble reliance on God in His Word, that is to say faith, is the immediate way to receive remission and new life. I dare to say that he was true to the Prophets and Apostles in not only saying these things but placing them in the foreground of his teaching.

But we have followed Simeon to his College through the gathering shadows of that Sunday evening of September. He has walked up Market Street, and across or along the then contracted Market Place, and past St. Mary's Church, perhaps with a thought of his approaching turn as preacher there; and so beneath the gateway of King's, and across the lawn of that majestic Court, and up by 'The Saint's Rest' to his quiet rooms. He will never take that walk again.

Chapter 15

Death and Burial

Mr Carus devotes many pages to the last few weeks of Simeon's life. So vivid and affecting is the record which he preserves, written not by himself, but by an anonymous friend of Simeon's, who was his 'constant attendant' to the last, that I make no apology for giving a proportionate space in this little book to the story of those days. It shall be told mainly in the word of the original 'Narrative'.

On the Tuesday (September 20) he was in high health and spirits, and talked of the journey he proposed to make the next day to Ely with no ordinary delight. In conversation however at this time with his friend he made the following remarks about his nearness to the eternal world: 'Well, though I am talking of putting by things for my journey to Bath next June, the Lord knows that I am thinking, and longing to a certain degree, for a far better journey, which in a few days I shall take; but I find it difficult to realise the thought that I am so near the eternal world. I cannot imagine what a spirit is; I have no conception of it. But I rejoice in the thought that my coffin is already cut down, and in the town at this very time; of this I have no doubt; – and my shroud is also ready, and in a few days I shall join the company of the redeemed above.'

His friend replied, 'Why, dear Sir, should you talk so? You are in good health and strength; and November is so near; I think you will be permitted to preach your sermons, and also to prepare the other set you are thinking of; and perhaps you may preach them too.'

He said, 'That will be as the Lord pleases; but I do often wonder at the degree of strength and spirits which of late He has blessed me with. I never remember to have had greater energy for work than at this time; and I do seem to think that it is the Lord's will to spare me through November. But you know it is quite immaterial to me; the

183

sermons are finished, that is all I care about. But if I should be permitted to preach them, I expect it will bring me down; indeed, I give
you all leave to break all my bones in December. Still I am fully
determined, if I have any degree of strength left, instantly to begin a
set of sermons on that grand subject out of Ephesians, 3rd chapter,
18th and 19th verses. I don't expect or desire to preach them; but if
my life be spared, write them I will.'

The next day, Wednesday, September 21, he went over to Ely, to
pay his respects to the new bishop, Dr. Allen. He had been very
anxious about this visit; for, as he was one of the oldest of the clergy,
it was his wish, he said, to be among the very first to show all respect to his diocesan. The day was damp and chilly, and he needed
more than usual care to prevent any injurious effects from the journey; but he felt so strong and vigorous that he imprudently dispensed
with his ordinary outer dress. The Bishop received him with marked
kindness and attention, and proposed that they should go together
to see the cathedral. Here they lingered too long; the coldness of
the building, increased by the rawness of the day, soon began sensi-
bly to affect him, and was the direct cause of the illness from which
he never recovered.

Saturday, September 24, was his birthday. Though he had passed
but an indifferent night, he rose early this morning, and, when his
attendant came to him, he was sitting in a favourite spot before the
window, to enjoy the first beams of the sun, and employed in writing a letter. Referring to his journey to Ely he remarked, 'If this is
to be the closing scene, I shall not at all regret my journey to the
Bishop.'

For some days he remained in much the same state; but subse-
quently so far recovered that occasionally he could take a drive in
his carriage, and we began to indulge a hope of his recovery. On
October 6 he dictated a letter which exhibits all his usual precision
on subjects which deeply interested him.

It was a letter to a friend who proposed to build a church
at Jerusalem. He praises the zeal and hope, but advises patience most of all: 'I am never in danger but when acting; all
goes well with me when I am in a passive state – I am then

saying, Lord, what wilt Thou have me to do? ... In acting there is pleasure; in waiting there is self-denial; but in assuring ourselves that God in due season will make our way clear there is exquisite delight.'

But he ventured on a drive one damp and chilly day, and all the malady returned. He recognised at once and decisively the message of death, and hastened to complete his will. His whole property was £5,000.[1] This he left, except for a few small legacies, to his Trust Fund, and then 'prepared himself with joy for his departure'.

On Friday, October 21, the last hopes of his friends were gone. But he 'seemed more than usually calm and happy'. His friend, sitting by his bed, asked him what he was just then thinking of. He answered, full of animation, 'I don't *think* now; I am *enjoying*'; and then spoke of his entire surrender to the will of God, and of the gladness of it; adding with peculiar emphasis, 'He cannot do anything against my will'.

All trace of the old infirmities of temper was gone in those last suffering weeks. A respectable person, who was much about Simeon at the time, told me, some fifteen years ago, that he watched the old man's absolute patience day by day in the sick-room with reverence and wonder; it was as if he could not be impatient. He was at perfect rest in the will of God.

His smiles were always singularly bright, but now more bright than ever. Words came slowly, with long pauses, and often in clear whispers. 'Infinite wisdom has arranged the whole with infinite love; and infinite power enables me – to rest upon that love.' 'I am in a dear Father's hands – all is

---

1. Of the £15,000 inherited from his brother he had already transferred £10,000 to his nephew, Sir R.G. Simeon, when he was returned in 1832 as M.P. for the Isle of Wight.

secure. When I look to Him (he spoke with singular solemnity), I see nothing but faithfulness – and immutability – and truth; and I have the sweetest peace – *I cannot have more peace*. But if I look another way – to the poor creature – O then there is nothing – nothing – but what is to be abhorred and mourned over.'

'Nothing could exceed the calmness and dignity both of his spirit and manner.' At one moment, when it was thought the end had come, several attendants, with the doctor (Dr. Haviland) and Mr. Carus, gathered round him. He gravely protested: 'You want to see what is called a dying scene. That I abhor from my inmost soul. I wish to be alone, with my God, the lowest of the low.'

His faith reposed itself on the revelation of our redemption in its harmony and unity:

'Yes,' said he, 'it is upon the broad grand principles of the Gospel that I repose – it is not upon any particular promise here or there – any little portions of the Word, which some people seem to take comfort from; but I wish to look at the *grand whole* – at the vast scheme of redemption as from eternity to eternity. Indeed to say the truth, what may be called my spiritual exercises have lately been at rather a low ebb ... but however that may be, I am not solicitous so much about this feeling or that, as upon keeping before me the grand purposes of Jehovah from eternity to eternity. I might wish to be able to go forth and survey all the glories of heaven and the blessedness of that place; there might however be something in all that to be suspected. But in taking the great revelation of Himself which God has given us, *there* I rest upon *Him*, and not upon myself, and so I remain' ...

I quoted the passage, 'I am the Lord, I change not, therefore ye sons of Jacob are not consumed.'

'Yes; that is the true view of the matter as it appears to me. For after all what are a man's thoughts before *Him*? It cannot depend upon a few poor, broken, puling words; nor do I depend upon these

... I take the glorious and majestic discoveries which God has made to me of Himself, and there I rest.'

He then added, smiling as he used to do when making some strong statement upon any point about which he himself had not the slightest doubt: 'I may be wrong in my view – though I think I am not'; – then very solemnly and slowly, 'But, however, this I know, that I am the chief of sinners, and the greatest monument of God's mercy; and I know *I cannot be wrong here.*'

Again the illness ebbed, and on October 27 he was occupied in 'perfecting a scheme for four sermons upon his favourite passage', the wonderful words which close the third chapter to the Ephesians. He dictated a brief, suggestive outline of exposition; correcting and improving as he went. He said, 'I should think a life well spent, out of heaven, to write upon that passage in a manner worthy of it.'

Soon afterwards he dictated the short address on the Missions to the Jews which I have quoted above; and then, a little later, a solemn entreaty that he might never again be allowed to hear reported a word of human praise of himself.

On November 3 he had a cordial letter from Bishop Allen, telling him that the last great desire of his heart was granted, the appointment of Mr. Carus to succeed him in his church.

On the evening of this day we thought he was beginning to lose his consciousness of what was passing, as he no longer took notice of anything, and his eyes had been closed for many hours. Suddenly, however, he remarked, 'If you want to do what I am doing, go and look in the first chapter of the Ephesians from the third to the fourteenth verse; there you will see what I am enjoying now.' This was the last chapter which he requested to have read to him; but such was his weakness, that it was only when read in a whisper that he could bear to hear it. Another kindred passage of Scripture, the last verse of the eleventh of Romans, was one on which he would dwell for hours together, repeating the words, 'For *of* Him – and *through* Him – and *to* Him are all things; to whom be glory.'

The next day, November 4, he drank a little wine pre-
scribed for him. It happened to be some of the sort called
Lacryma Christi, sent him by a friend. 'Stretching forth his
feeble and withered arms in the attitude of prayer, he began
to invoke a blessing on all present: "May all the blessings
which my adorable Saviour purchased for me with His *tears*,
yea with His own precious life-blood, be now given me to
enjoy, and to my two dearest friends, Sir Richard (his nephew)
and Mr. Carus, and my two dear nurses (his niece, Lady Baker,
and the writer), and to that dear friend who gave me this
wine – that they may enjoy the same in time and eternity."....
Afterwards, referring to what had passed, he observed,
"There! I shall drink no more of that *wine* until I drink it *new*
(that word he uttered in a peculiarly significant tone) with
my Redeemer in His kingdom."'

Early in his illness, 'when we asked him if he would like
to take medicine, or wait, he used to say, "Why do you ask
me what I like? I am the Lord's patient, I cannot but like
everything; don't say, Will you do this, or that? but say, Here
is this; you must take that; *I like everything*." When we expressed our sorrow once that he had passed a wakeful night,
he replied with a remarkable expression of contentment on
his venerable countenance, "Never mind; *He* giveth His beloved sleep." At another time he said, "I shall never sleep
until I fall asleep in the arms of Jesus Christ." On one occasion when I had bathed his eyes, and asked him if they were
relieved, he said, opening them and looking up to heaven,
"Soon they will behold all the glorified saints and angels
around the throne of my God and Saviour, who has loved me
unto death, and given Himself for me; then I shall see Him
whom having not seen I love; in whom, though I see not, yet
believing I rejoice with joy unspeakable and full of glory";

and turning his eyes towards me, he added, "Of the reality of this I am as sure as I were there this moment."'

For the very last few days he suffered grievously, and could scarcely whisper. 'Jesus Christ is all in all for my soul,' he said to his friend, 'and now you must be all for my body. I cannot tell you any longer what I want.' But thought as well as faith remained firm: 'My principles were not founded on fancies or enthusiasm; there is a reality in them, and I find them sufficient to support me in death.'

On Friday afternoon, November 11, with a great effort, and without a word, he folded his hands for the last time in the attitude of prayer, and then stretched them out as in farewell to his friends. His last utterance was made that night, a faint *Amen* in answer to the Aaronic benediction. All through the Saturday he lay unconscious and without motion. On Sunday, November 13, at ten minutes after two o'clock, when the bell of St. Mary's, not far off, had just ceased to call the congregation to the University Sermon (it should have been the second sermon of his own course), he struggled for a moment, and then rested with his Lord.

'When Mr Valiant-for-Truth understood the summons, he called for his friends, and told them of it. Then said he, "I am going to my Father's; and though with great difficulty I have got hither, yet now I do not repent me of all the troubles I have been at to arrive where I am." When the day that he must go hence was come, many accompanied him to the river side; into which as he went he said, "Death, where is thy sting?" And as he went down deeper he said, "Grave where is thy victory?" So he passed over, and all the trumpets sounded for him on the other side.'

Simeon's will was opened, and was found to contain a mention of his desired place of burial: 'If I die out of College, I am not careful where my body shall be buried. But if I die in Cambridge, I should wish to be buried in my College Chapel.' And preparations were made to lay him in the great vault beneath the antechapel pavement.

King's College Chapel, the place of that memorable funeral, one of the chief glories of English architecture, is so often visited, and so widely known by prints and photographs, that it needs no elaborate description here. Its vast 'fan-vaulted' roof, nearly three hundred feet long and forty broad, hangs with all its weight of sculptured stone eighty feet above the floor, sustained without on either side by eleven huge but graceful buttresses. At the angles of the structure rise four lofty towers, till within recent years the one familiar landmark of Cambridge across the ample plain. Henry the Sixth began the building, but the Wars of the Roses delayed its completion till the latter years of Henry the Seventh, and his son saw the last additions given to the internal ornaments – the massive organ-screen, once the rood-loft, carved by Italian hands with all the grotesque beauty of the Renaissance, and the wonderful windows, twenty-six in number, filled with painted glass, 'good, clene, sure and perfyte', as the ancient specification runs. In them 'the story of the olde lawe and of the newe lawe' is depicted 'in oryent colours and imagery', almost wholly on the designs and by the hands of English 'glasyers', but in such style as to have suggested untenable conjectures that Dürer, or Holbein, or even Raphael, was directly concerned. As the visitor or worshipper receives the impressions of that solemn temple, whether as the sun fills it in summer, or the faint light of the many tapers in the stalls makes the aerial darkness visible in the winter afternoon, while sound calls out all the soul of form, he thinks it no wonder that such art suggested to the great Poet of Nature one of his noblest sonnets:

> Give all thou canst; high Heaven rejects the lore
> Of nicely calculated less or more:
> So deem'd the man who fashion'd for the sense
> These lofty pillars, spread that branching roof
> Self-poised, and scoop'd into ten thousand cells,
> Where light and shade repose, where music dwells
> Lingering and wandering on as loth to die –
> Like thoughts whose very sweetness yieldeth proof
> That they were born for immortality.

Simeon had 'loved the habitation' of this house of God. There he had received the blessed Bread and Wine on that happy Easter Day of his first year in college, and there he had learnt to find the prayers, psalms, and lessons sweet to his soul. Now his body was to rest in its keeping till our temporal sanctuaries shall no longer be needed.

The funeral was not designedly public; Simeon had desired that it should be very simple. Many of his clerical friends had expressed a strong wish to be present, and they received a notice of the day; and the Provost gave private admission into the antechapel to the congregation of Trinity Church; but otherwise no outside attendance was officially supposed. However, the whole University was resolved to honour this man, once almost banished from its society; and 'the funeral unavoidedly became one altogether of a public character'. Heads of Houses, Doctors, Professors, men of all ages, stations and opinions, and of every college, came to the burial of Simeon.

It was Saturday, November 19, and the town was busy with the market; but all the shops in the main street were shut,

and the iron railings east and north of the College were beset
by dense crowds of people. In the University and Colleges
almost every lecture that morning was suspended, that all
who would might go to the grave.

It is no dishonour to other illustrious names to say that
probably Cambridge never saw quite such a funeral as Simeon's; for not only was the attendance vast and the respect
profound, but countless hearts felt that they had lost a father,
and all remembered the contrasts of the former days.

The coffin was brought down those familiar stairs to the
Hall, and thence the procession set out, under a sad November sky. The Choristers, Scholars, and Fellows walked first;
immediately in front of the bier, the Provost, George
Thackeray; behind it, Sir Richard Simeon, the chief mourner;
and the eight Senior Fellows bore the pall of their brother.
Dr. Francis Close, a Dean of Carlisle, writes of the funeral
thus:

> The like of it was never seen, nor ever will be seen again. More than
> 1500 gownsmen attended to honour a man who had been greatly
> despised. When his venerable remains were deposited in that glori-
> ous building, every bell of the College Chapels tolled for him, and
> the Vice-Chancellor (Ainslie, Master of Pembroke) regretted that
> the great bell of St. Mary's could not, as its use was confined to the
> Royal Family, or to a Vice-Chancellor dying in office. Such was the
> honour the great King was pleased to bestow upon his servant ....
> 'And they glorified God in him.'

No monument within the Chapel celebrates Simeon's name;
such records are not placed there, except a few in the side-
chapels. But just above the site of the coffin the two letters
'C.S.', and the date '1836', have been cut in the floor and
filled with lead.

In his Church a memorial was soon afterwards erected by

the congregation, a large decorated tablet, affixed to the chancel wall, close to the stones which commemorate the names and labours of his beloved Martyn and Thomason. It bears a short inscription, suggested in substance by himself:

In Memory of
THE REV. CHARLES SIMEON, M.A.,
SENIOR FELLOW OF KING'S COLLEGE,
AND FIFTY-FOUR YEARS VICAR OF THIS PARISH; WHO,
WHETHER AS THE GROUND OF HIS OWN HOPES,
OR AS
THE SUBJECT OF ALL HIS MINISTRATIONS,
DETERMINED
TO KNOW NOTHING BUT
JESUS CHRIST AND HIM CRUCIFIED.
1 Cor. 2:2

APPENDIX

A Selection from Simeon's Correspondence

Simeon's correspondence was no small part of his work at Cambridge. Canon Carus has preserved a large number of the letters in his admirable Memoir; indeed the Second Part of it consists entirely of a careful arrangement of letters. And I have already put a good many extracts from these before the reader. But let me add here a sheaf of specimens from Simeon's letters of counsel. Seldom surely has the post been better used than by him in these silent labours of love and wisdom.

To a young Clergyman; January 1792:

'My dear friend, walk close with God; it is the only way to be either safe or happy. Live retired – read much – pray much – abound in all offices of love – shun the company that may draw you aside – seek the company of those from whom you may receive edification in your soul – be dying daily to the world – consider yourself as a soldier that is not to be "entangled with the things of this life, in order that you may please Him who hath chosen you to be a soldier"; finally, "be faithful unto death, and Christ will give thee a crown of life."'

To the same, a little later. He writes of what he knows:

'One who did not speak at random has said that he esteemed the reproach of Christ as greater riches than all the treasures in Egypt. Such too will you find it, if you can only take up the cross. It is our great aversion to the cross that makes it burdensome; when we have learned to glory in it, we have found the philosopher's stone. When we are enabled to say with Paul, "Most gladly will I rather glory in my infirmities, that the power of Christ may rest upon me; therefore I take pleasure in infirmities, in reproaches, in necessities, in persecutions, in distresses for Christ's sake"; when, I say, we are like-minded with Paul in this respect, we have learned to explain a more difficult riddle than ever Samson's was. But, till we have been taught this lesson, nothing can be done to any good purpose.... It is remarkable that our Lord has laid this at the threshold which we must pass in order to follow Him one single step; "If any man will be My disciple, let him deny himself, and take up his cross, and follow Me."'.

To a Friend, who was in trouble with his Bishop. A different side of Christian duty is in view here:

March 7, 1814.
'My Dear Friend,
Circumstanced as you are, I feel no hesitation in saying that you should avoid everything that can give offence, except the faithful preaching of "Christ crucified". Why should you stand out about the Hymns? You are very injudicious in this. You should consider that, when a storm is raised, you are not the only sufferer. Pray study to maintain peace, though you make some sacrifices for it. I stated that your pamphlet was "somewhat objectionable"; but, if I had not been afraid of wounding your feelings, I should have said, "*very* objectionable".... You are not aware that, whilst you are afraid of being thought to act from the fear of man, you are actually under its influence; only it is the religious that you fear instead of the irreligious .... This in few words is my advice: first, Preach faithfully, but speak the truth *in love*; second, Do all the good you can in visiting your parish, but don't exercise any pastoral function out of it; third, Put aside Hymns, which are quite unnecessary; fourth, Do not attempt to go to the utmost of what the law allows about private meetings; fifth, Be as quiet as possible, and let the storm blow over. Observe especially, I do not give this as advice to all persons, in all circumstances, but to you in your circumstances. You have given your enemies great advantage against you .... You have evidently some very injudicious advisers about you. Be content to let your conduct be misinterpreted for a season. Be as regular as possible in every-

thing; and in a year or two your enemies will be put to silence. Do not be anxious about preaching in other churches, and going to prisons. Labour in your own proper sphere as diligently as you will. Above all, do not shift blame from yourself on your patron. If non-parishioners came to the Lord's Table, it is not your place to repel them: that belongs to the churchwardens. And if they choose to do it under present circumstances, recommend the people not to come. It will all blow over soon. I am much afflicted on your account, and shall feel comforted in an assurance that you will retire to your castle, which is impregnable, and not by injudicious sallies expose yourself to unnecessary difficulties and dangers. I am, dear Sir, most affectionately yours.

A correspondent had asked his advice about the choice of a college for a younger brother:

K.C., November 1, 1816.
'My dear Sir,
There are many reasons why I should prefer – for your brother before any other college. He will find there a greater variety of religious characters than elsewhere, and will therefore more easily fall into the habits of those who are prudent, whilst his little singularities will be the less noticed. But if he go about visiting the sick instead of attending to his academical studies, I shall give my voice against him instantly that he may be removed: and if he come to college, he must come with the express understanding that he shall be removed upon the first intimation from the Tutor, and not be continued, to be dismissed by authority. If he come without a full determination to conform in all things to college discipline and college studies, or with any idea of acting here as he might in a little country parish, he will do incalculable injury to religion. Pray let him understand this, and not come at all, if he is not prepared both to submit to authority and to follow friendly advice.'

A 'Simeonite' undergraduate had been suspected of writing some foolish remarks in a book belonging to his College Library, and would not confess it. Simeon's letter is severe, but not too severe; it is a good example of his jealousy for thorough practical consistency in those who 'professed religion':

December 14, 1810.
'SIR,
In your letter to me you say, "you never wrote such a paragraph to your knowledge." You have nothing to do but to write down the same words, and you will soon see, on a comparison of the handwriting, whether you wrote it or not. It is evident you have been in the habit of writing in the books of the College Library. This, not to speak of the presumption, is a most flagrant breach of confidence, and deserves the most serious reprehension. What if every undergraduate took the same liberty? If your conduct excited prejudice only against yourself, I should think that I had little to do with it, except in a way of private advice; but it involves the whole body of religious young men, and religion itself together with them; and therefore calls for a public testimony of my disapprobation. You are not at all aware how contrary your conduct in this matter has been to the modesty that becomes a young man, and a religious professor in particular: and I hope you will take occasion from it to mark how exceedingly defective you are in that prime ornament of a Christian character. My advice is that you compare your handwriting with the paragraph in question, in order to refresh your memory; and that, when you have found out the extent of your misconduct, you go to your Tutor, and confess it, and humble yourself for it. When you have done that, and obtained forgiveness of your college, I shall be happy to see you again upon the former footing.'

A lady had asked him about a question of conscience about duty to her husband:

'I will lay down some principles, and then suggest how, in my opinion, they should be modified in the application.
    'First, We must serve God faithfully and supremely.
    'Second, We must serve men faithfully, but in subordination to God, and so far only as will consist with our duty to God.
    'But firstly, we must take care not to make that sin which is not sin, or that duty which is not duty: the former of these is needless scrupulosity; the latter is superstition.

'Secondly, we must take care not to make that *our* duty which is the duty of others indeed, but not ours; for instance, as in the State there may be many things amiss, which yet it is not *our* duty, but the duty of Parliament only, to rectify, so there may be in the house of a husband. A wife may advise, but not order, except in *her own* department. You may lament evil, but not authoritatively oppose it, where God has not invested you with the supreme command.

'Thirdly, we must distinguish between things evil *in themselves*, and things evil *by accident* only.... It would take me too long to assign all my reasons; reasons enough will occur to you. If I considered your welfare alone, I should say, "Renounce such vanities altogether"; for in your state of mind I doubt not but that they have a great tendency to injure your spiritual and eternal interests; but your husband's welfare ought to be most dear both to you and me: and consequently such a line of conduct as is most kind and conciliatory, and likely to win him, is that which I should advise.

'But if you find him fixed and determined, yield instantly without uttering a word. Let your compliance be kind and affectionate, however opposite it be to your own wishes. Let any differences of opinion between you and your husband be revealed to none, without absolute necessity; and be extremely careful whom you consult. It is not every one that is able to advise. It is easy enough to lay down general principles, but to modify them to existing circumstances is extremely difficult. In this consists the difference between a novice and a father, between folly and wisdom, error and truth.'

He writes to 'one who had been urged to preach very strongly':

December 7, 1817.
'What is your object? Is it to *win* souls? If it be, how are you to set about it? By exciting all manner of prejudices, and driving people from the church? How did our Lord act? He spake the words in parables *as men were able to hear it*. How did St. Paul act? He fed the babes with *milk*, and not with strong meat. As for the religious world, they are as selfish, for the most part, as the ignorant and ungodly. They are not content that you should seek the welfare of others, unless you, *to please them*, bring forward also things which

will utterly subvert your end; and if they be but gratified, they care not who is stumbled and driven away.

'You must not be in bondage to the religious world any more than to the ungodly. True, you are not to keep back the fundamental doctrines of the Gospel, but there are different ways of stating them; and you should adopt that which expresses kindness and love, and not that which indicates an unfeeling harshness. Only speak from love to man, and not from the fear of man, and God will both accept and prosper you.'

To another, on Christian expediency:

December 10, 1817.
'My Dear Friend,
I should be cautious of making up my mind *strongly* on anything that is not clearly defined in Scripture. Nothing is easier than to lay down an apparently good principle, and to err in following it, *e.g.* the eating of meats offered to idols, and circumcision. Do not make bonds for your own feet; constructed as your mind is, you will be in danger of this. In things that are good or evil *per se*, there is no room for expediency; in things that are good or evil only *by accident*, expediency must guide you. Many think that the opposite to right must be wrong; but the opposite to right may be right, as in the instance before specified. The human mind is very fond of fetters, and is apt to forge them for itself. This is not, however, recommended by
          Your very affectionate Friend and Brother in the Lord.'

To a Curate, who had been requested by his Incumbent to leave him:

March 18, 1819.
'I never interfere in the concerns of others, unless called to do so by both parties. As an abstract question, I think that for a man professing piety to force himself upon his principal against his will is no very Christian act. There are a set of people in the Church who would recommend and encourage such a step; but they are not the most humble and modest of our flock. You must take care what spirit

you encourage in others, and what spirit you exercise yourself. I
am, dear Sir,

Your most faithful servant,
C.S.'

To a Missionary, on the religion of personal experience:

'Your letter shows me what I was most anxious to hear, that you are
growing in self-knowledge; and it therefore opens to me a fit opportunity of declaring to you what have been my fears respecting
you from the beginning. You have always appeared to me to be sin-
.cere. But your views of Christianity seemed to be essentially defective. You have always appeared to admire Christianity *as a system*; but you never seemed to have just views of Christianity *as a
remedy*; you never seemed to possess self-knowledge, or to know
the evil of your own heart. I never saw in you any deep contrition,
much less anything of a tender self-loathing and self-abhorrence.
This always made me jealous over you with a godly jealousy; and
never till this moment have I had my fears for your ultimate state
removed. I beheld in you somewhat of a child-like simplicity; and I
well know that, *if it be associated with contrition*, it is a virtue of
the sublimest quality; but if contrition be wanting, the disposition
which assumes that form differs but little from childishness.

'You may conceive the brazen serpent which Moses erected in
the wilderness to have been exquisitely formed, and you may suppose persons to have greatly admired the workmanship, and the con-
trivance of erecting it upon a pole for the benefit of all who should
behold it; but the meanest person in the whole camp, who had but
the most indistinct view of it, if he beheld it with a sense of his own
dying condition, and with an experience of its efficacy to heal his
wounds, would have an incomparably better view of it than the vir-
tuoso, however much he might admire it. This hint will show you
what in my judgment you *were*, and what I hope you *will* be. Christianity is a personal matter, not to be commended merely to others,
but to be experienced in your own soul: and though you may con-
found your opponents by your arguments, you will never do any
essential good, and much less will you reap any saving benefit to
your own soul, till you can say, "What mine eyes have seen, mine

ears have heard, and mine hands have handled of the word of life, that same declare I unto you".'

To the Hon. H. Ryder, Dean of Wells, on his election to the see of Gloucester; May, 1815.

'You have hitherto seen religion as it exists in a Wilberforce and a Babington; but you will now have to behold it with many sad mixtures of human infirmity. Sometimes it will require a great degree of charity to admit its existence at all; as when it shall appear connected with disingenuousness and duplicity. And where its existence cannot well be doubted, it will often be found to operate to a far less extent than might be reasonably expected. Its effects are very gradual; it does not leaven the whole lump at once; it will not immediately give wisdom to one who is naturally weak, or prudence to one of a sanguine temperament, or meekness to one who is naturally bold and forward. The very circumstance of its operating powerfully on the human mind will frequently occasion it to produce an unfavourable course of action, where the judgment is not sufficiently enlightened to decide between apparently opposite and conflicting duties. All this, and more, you will now have to see, to feel, to regulate, to correct; and, after all your labours, you will have little else from man than a comment on that proverb (to which you are already no stranger), *Bene facere et male audire regium est.*

'Nor will you be without trials even from some of your dearest friends: for piety is not always attended with discretion; and you may be sometimes urged to things which, though desirable in themselves, are not expedient; and if you will not see with their eyes they may manifest, in a way painful to your feelings, their disappointment and chagrin; and constrain you to seek your comfort in the testimony of your own conscience and in the approbation of your God.'

To a Friend, on maintaining charity:

'In order to form a correct judgment of your spirit, ask yourself what you should think of a person who should speak in the same acrimonious way of you? You would doubtless condemn him for his uncharitableness. You would tell him that, even if there were some just fault to be found, *love* would rather cover it, and would hope that the conduct was not so bad as it appeared. Then let this be your own spirit towards others. I do indeed make great allowances for you; for it is not easy for a person, noticed and caressed as you are, to preserve a humble spirit. But humility and love are the chief ornaments of a Christian; and if you decline in these, God will leave you to fall into some dreadful sin, and constrain you to learn by bitter experience what you do not learn in a season of prosperity.

'Write me word that you take these suggestions kindly and thankfully at my hands. Write me word that you have spread the matter before the Lord in prayer, and that He has discovered to you your error in indulging so uncharitable a spirit. And then I shall bless God that I have taken up my pen to speak, at the risk of being accounted "an enemy for telling you the truth."

Your very affectionate Friend.'

Incidents of his preaching-work during his invalid period, told in a letter to Thomason:

K.C., July 15, 1817.
'My Beloved Brother,
... I see very little company of any kind. I find that silence, perfect silence, is the only thing for me; and by imposing that upon myself at all other times, I go through my public duty with energy and comfort. Last year during the Long Vacation I took the First Epistle to the Thessalonians for my subject on Sunday mornings, and through mercy was enabled not only to enter into the spirit of it, but to *breathe* the spirit of it in my ministrations. But the proud, unsubdued spirit of some of my people could not bear it. Had I scolded them from the pulpit, they could have endured it: but when I wept over them, and besought them with many tears, they quite raged, and separated from me altogether. But those who were of a humbler spirit were twined closer round my heart. *Now* the Second Epistle to the Corinthians comes in its proper order; and I am entering upon it with great delight. The first twelve verses of the second chapter will be my subject next Sunday morning. My soul longs to drink into the spirit of the Apostle, if peradventure I may recover and

restore those who yet attend my ministry. At all events, I find it sweet to have the testimony of my own conscience that I desire no other office than to be "a helper of their joy." I am labouring this point also with all my little might in private, that so I may leave them all without excuse, if they return not to me as children to a loving parent.'

He writes, October, 1821, to the Rev. J. W. Cunningham, on some recent writings of Chalmers, for whom he expresses a warm admiration:

'I think he carries too far the complaint about Government making use of ministers (of religion) in secular matters. Dr. C. and half a score of others may find it a serious inconvenience. The great mass of ministers, I fear, throughout the United Kingdom would not engage one atom more in spiritual exercises, or in ministerial labours, if they were to be exempted from all temporal matters tomorrow. Still, if some things are overstrained (and who ever rode a favourite hobby without going now and then a little too fast?), many things are nobly stated and come with great power to the mind; and I rejoice exceedingly that you are calling the attention of the public to them .... Religious people are apt to overlook secular matters, instead of giving them a due measure of attention, forgetting that motto, *Nihil humani a me alienum puto* ....

'My province is just to attend to the little things that are before me. Were I to attempt to execute Dr. C.'s plans, my folly would soon appear unto all men. I have often thought that, as *sapientia prima est stultitia caruisse*, so *secunda est* to know *quid valeant humeri, quid ferre recusent*; and however defective in the first, I have studied carefully, and to pretty good purpose, the second.'

To the Rev. Edward Elliott, of Brighton, just bereaved of his wife:

'I often think that my mind is very peculiarly constructed in this respect, that the death of those who are dear to me is in many cases a real source of joy, from the realising view which I have of their happiness. But a few days ago, a relation of Mr. Scott was regretting that he was drawing near his closing scene: and so far was I from sympathising with him in his regret, that I could not refrain from congratulating the departing saint on his prospects. I say the same in reference to dear P.

'Yet whilst I say this, I mean not that the feelings of nature should be suppressed, but sanctified, and elevated to a heavenly refinement. And I feel assured that such will be the one sentiment that will pervade you all, when assembled on the mournful occasion of committing her mortal remains to the tomb. I even now *taste* the spirit of you all: I seem to be one with you all: I think I understand you all: and you also understand me. I *love* the "gathering into stillness," the sweet sorrow, and the adoring joy.'

To the same (he is referring to Mr. Elliott's grandfather, Henry Venn of Yelling):

'How far this may be connected with a principle which for more than forty years I have laboured diligently to cultivate, I know not. It has been a favourite object with me, as far as human weakness would admit of it, to love all for my Saviour's sake, and in proportion as I have seen, or thought I saw, His image in them. And it may possibly be that the fixedness of this principle in my mind, as it respects my Saviour, has led me into an error with respect to him whom I have ever loved, next to my Saviour. Be it so; and, if it be a fault, forgive it. But it will take some time, after all, to convince me that the feelings of love and gratitude to a departed saint can be too ardent, or that a thought of exultation, when I find my arm long enough to reach him, is bad.'

A personal statement:

K.C., December 19, 1821.
'A circumstance has just occurred; and I record it merely to illustrate an idea long familiar to my mind, and brought home to my experience, if not every day, certainly every *week* of my life; viz., that the servant of God does not live under the same laws as others; and that if he were to act towards others as they do towards him, the world, who are regardless of the treatment he meets with, would be

full of indignation against him. (The incident is then narrated.)

'Perhaps I ought to take some notice of it; but my rule is – never to hear, or see, or know, what if heard, or seen, or known, would call for animadversion from me. Hence it is that I dwell in peace in the midst of lions. My blessed Lord, "when He was reviled, reviled not again; when He suffered, He threatened not, but committed Himself to Him that judgeth righteously." That seems the right thing for me to do; though some perhaps would think it better for me to stand up for my rights. But to all the accusations that were brought against Him, our Lord made no reply, *insomuch that the governor marvelled greatly.* I delight in that record: and God helping me, it is the labour of my life so to act that on *my* account also the governor, or spectator, may marvel greatly.

'My experience all this day has been, and I hope will yet continue to be, a confirmation of that word, "Thou wilt hide me in the secret of thy presence from the strife of tongues." Insult an Angel before the throne; and what would he care about it? Just such will be my feeling, whilst I am *hid in the secret* of my Redeemer's presence.'

To Mrs. Cunningham, 1827:

'I am in the habit of accounting religion as the simplest of all concerns: – "To Him that loved us, and washed us from our sins in His own blood, and hath made us kings and priests unto our God, to Him be glory and dominion for ever and ever," expresses the very frame of mind in which I wish both to live and die ...

'I have been just interrupted by a clergyman, a Fellow of – College, who has begun to seek after the Lord, and who came to introduce himself to me. I know not what he must think of me with my eyes suffused with tears; but I trust he found my spirit sweetly softened and affectionately solicitous for his welfare.'

He tells Thomason (1812) his own thoughts about correspondence:

'As for sitting down to write a religious letter, it is what I cannot do myself, and what I do not very much admire, unless there be some particular occasion that calls for it. I love rather that a letter be a free and easy communication of such things as are upon the mind, and such as we imagine will interest the person with whom we correspond. Some indeed, who have a talent for letter writing, may employ their pen profitably in the more direct and formal way; but it is a thing I cannot do; religion with me is only the salt with which I season the different subjects on which I write; and it is recommended in that view by St. Paul, to be used in the whole of our converse with each other.'

INDEX OF PERSONS

Other biographies published by
Christian Focus Publications
in the Historymakers series

Thomas Boston by Andrew Thomson
Henry Havelock by John Pollock
Pastor Hsi by Geraldine Taylor
Martin Luther by Thomas Lindsay
Robert Murray McCheyne by Alexander Smellie
Moody Without Sankey by John Pollock
George Muller by Roger Steer
John Newton by Richard Cecil
John Owen by Andrew Thomson
Hudson (Taylor) and Maria by John Pollock